Brain Tumors

Titles in the Diseases and Disorders series include:

Acne
AIDS
Alzheimer's Disease
Anorexia and Bulimia
Anthrax
Arthritis
Asthma
Attention Deficit Disorder
Autism
Bipolar Disorder
Birth Defects
Breast Cancer
Cerebral Palsy
Chronic Fatigue Syndrome
Cystic Fibrosis
Deafness
Diabetes
Down Syndrome
Dyslexia
Epilepsy
Fetal Alcohol Syndrome
Food Poisoning
Headaches

Heart Disease
Hemophilia
Hepatitis
Leukemia
Lou Gehrig's Disease
Lyme Disease
Mad Cow Disease
Malaria
Measles and Rubella
Multiple Sclerosis
Obesity
Ovarian Cancer
Parkinson's Disease
Phobias
SARS
Schizophrenia
Sexually Transmitted
   Diseases
Sleep Disorders
Smallpox
Teen Depression
West Nile Virus

DISEASES & DISORDERS

Brain Tumors

Arda Darakjian Clark

LUCENT BOOKS

An imprint of Thomson Gale, a part of The Thomson Corporation

Detroit • New York • San Francisco • San Diego • New Haven, Conn.
Waterville, Maine • London • Munich

On Cover: A colored magnetic resonance imaging (MRI) scan of a patient's brain shows the presence of a malignant brain tumor (in yellow, at left). The tumor has damaged the surrounding tissue (in red) and caused it to fill with fluid.

© 2006 Thomson Gale, a part of The Thomson Corporation.

Thomson and Star Logo are trademarks and Gale and Lucent Books are registered trademarks used herein under license.

For more information, contact
Lucent Books
27500 Drake Rd.
Farmington Hills, MI 48331-3535
Or you can visit our Internet site at http://www.gale.com

LIBRARY OF CONGRESS CATALOGING-IN-PUBLICATION DATA

Clark, Arda Darakjian, 1956–
   Brain tumors / by Arda Darakjian Clark.
      p. cm. — (Diseases and disorders series)
Includes bibliographical references and index.
Contents: Understanding brain tumors—Diagnosis of brain tumors—Treatment of brain tumors—Follow-up care and rehabilitation—New trends in treatments.
ISBN 1-59018-671-0 (hardcover : alk paper) 1. Brain—Tumors—Juvenile literature. 2. Brain—Tumors—Treatment—Juvenile literature. I. Title. II. Series.
   RC280.B7C49 2006
   616.99'481—dc22
                                                                              2005018605

Printed in the United States of America

Table of Contents

Foreword 6

Introduction
 A Frightening Diagnosis 8

Chapter 1
 Understanding Brain Tumors 14

Chapter 2
 Diagnosis of Brain Tumors 30

Chapter 3
 Treatment of Brain Tumors 45

Chapter 4
 Follow-Up Care and Rehabilitation 60

Chapter 5
 New Trends in Treatment 75

Notes 90

Glossary 94

Organizations to Contact 97

For Further Reading 100

Works Consulted 102

Index 107

Picture Credits 111

About the Author 112

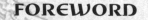

"The Most Difficult Puzzles Ever Devised"

Charles Best, one of the pioneers in the search for a cure for diabetes, once explained what it is about medical research that intrigued him so. "It's not just the gratification of knowing one is helping people," he confided, "although that probably is a more heroic and selfless motivation. Those feelings may enter in, but truly, what I find best is the feeling of going toe to toe with nature, of trying to solve the most difficult puzzles ever devised. The answers are there somewhere, those keys that will solve the puzzle and make the patient well. But how will those keys be found?"

Since the dawn of civilization, nothing has so puzzled people—and often frightened them, as well—as the onset of illness in a body or mind that had seemed healthy before. A seizure, the inability of a heart to pump, the sudden deterioration of muscle tone in a small child—being unable to reverse such conditions or even to understand why they occur was unspeakably frustrating to healers. Even before there were names for such conditions, even before they were understood at all, each was a reminder of how complex the human body was, and how vulnerable.

While our grappling with understanding diseases has been frustrating at times, it has also provided some of humankind's most heroic accomplishments. Alexander Fleming's accidental discovery in 1928 of a mold that could be turned into penicillin has resulted in the saving of untold millions of lives. The isolation of the enzyme insulin has reversed what was once a death sentence for anyone with diabetes. There have been great strides in combating conditions for which there is not yet a cure, too. Medicines can help AIDS patients live longer, diagnostic tools such as mammography and ultrasounds can help doctors find tumors while they are treatable, and laser surgery techniques have made the most intricate, minute operations routine.

This "toe-to-toe" competition with diseases and disorders is even more remarkable when seen in a historical continuum. An astonishing amount of progress has been made in a very short time. Just two hundred years ago, the existence of germs as a cause of some diseases was unknown. In fact, it was less than 150 years ago that a British surgeon named Joseph Lister had difficulty persuading his fellow doctors that washing their hands before delivering a baby might increase the chances of a healthy delivery (especially if they had just attended to a diseased patient)!

Each book in Lucent's Diseases and Disorders series explores a disease or disorder and the knowledge that has been accumulated (or discarded) by doctors through the years. Each book also examines the tools used for pinpointing a diagnosis, as well as the various means that are used to treat or cure a disease. Finally, new ideas are presented—techniques or medicines that may be on the horizon.

Frustration and disappointment are still part of medicine, for not every disease or condition can be cured or prevented. But the limitations of knowledge are being pushed outward constantly; the "most difficult puzzles ever devised" are finding challengers every day.

A Frightening Diagnosis

Day after day, Elaine Vega woke up with headaches. Some days the pressure in her head was so severe that she felt nauseated. When she consulted her doctor, he suspected that her symptoms were caused by a drug he had prescribed. Elaine had been taking the drug to prevent the recurrence of breast cancer, for which she had been treated a few years before.

The doctor changed her medication, but Elaine's headaches and nausea continued. To make things worse, Elaine began having seizures, brief episodes during which the muscles in her body would involuntarily jerk. Concerned that Elaine's symptoms were more than a reaction to her medication, Elaine's doctor ordered an imaging scan of her brain to see what might be causing the trouble. The scan showed that Elaine had seven tumors in her brain.

Elaine was one of more than 190,000 people who were diagnosed with brain tumors in the United States in 2004. While some of these patients' tumors grow from cells of the brain, most of them are formed when cells break off from tumors in other parts of the body, travel through the bloodstream to the brain, and form new tumors there. In Elaine's case, cells from her breast cancer had traveled to her brain and formed seven new tumors. Elaine began an intensive course of treatment to eradicate the tumors, but her disease was simply too aggressive and too advanced. She died less than six months after the diagnosis of the brain tumors.

Brain tumors are often fatal. As in Elaine's case, many patients die within months of diagnosis. More than two-thirds of adult patients and nearly one-third of children die within five years of diagnosis.

Despite grim outcomes like Elaine's, however, some patients do survive brain tumors. One famous survivor is champion bicyclist Lance Armstrong. In 1996, when he was twenty-five years old, Armstrong was diagnosed with cancer, which had begun as a tumor in one of his testicles and spread to his abdomen, lungs, and brain. Armstrong had surgery to remove the tumors. He also had chemotherapy to ensure that all cancer cells in his body were destroyed. Not only was Armstrong able to survive his cancer, but in 1999 he won the first of his seven consecutive victories in the Tour de France, bicycling's most prestigious competition.

A brain tumor (in red) is clearly visible in this color-enhanced diagnostic image. Nearly 200,000 Americans were diagnosed with brain tumors in 2004.

The Emotional Challenge of Brain Tumors

Although survival stories like Lance Armstrong's give hope to patients and doctors, the challenge posed by brain tumors is immense. The brain is the body's central governing organ. It controls all movements, thought, sensations, and emotions, as well as involuntary vital functions such as heartbeat and breathing. Therefore, tumors in the brain, which often disrupt these functions, pose serious threats to the patient's health and

In 1996 cyclist Lance Armstrong's testicular cancer spread to his brain as well as his abdomen and lungs. After successful treatment, he went on to win the Tour de France seven straight times.

survival. Furthermore, efforts to remove the tumors can be equally disruptive, limiting options for treatment. Being diagnosed with a brain tumor arouses strong emotional responses in patients and their families. Dr. Jimmie Holland, a psychiatrist who specializes in the care of cancer patients, writes, "The human side of illness is particularly poignant with reference to brain tumors. First, there is the fright and dread you feel when you're told that you have a brain tumor. How can you begin to adjust to such painful news? The diagnosis is a threat to your life, and also a threat to your 'thinking.' After all, our head is where we live."[1]

Patients with brain tumors typically experience a series of emotional responses to their diagnosis. These responses— shock, denial, guilt, anger, sadness, acceptance, and hope— have been identified by psychologists as common steps of coping with traumatic, life-altering events. Not all patients go through these emotional stages in the exact same order, but most of them experience at least some of these emotions.

The first typical response is shock. The mother of a young boy with a brain tumor describes her reaction when her son was diagnosed: "In 1991 I was a busy mother with three healthy children—and then my life changed forever. I learned that my then 7-year-old son Jay had a brain tumor. . . . The diagnosis of . . . brain tumor came as a shock. Cancer was something that happened to other people. Now, we were the other people."[2]

Patients and families find themselves in a circumstance for which they have had little or no preparation. As the aunt of a child with a brain tumor comments, "Newly diagnosed brain tumor patients are like people who don't know how to swim being thrown in deep water with no flotation device."[3]

Next, many patients deny their diagnosis. They may tell themselves that the doctor has made a mistake and that there is another and far less threatening explanation for their symptoms.

Once they come to accept the reality of a brain tumor, some patients may feel guilty for having somehow caused or contributed to the illness. Parents of children with brain tumors are especially likely to feel enormous guilt. The authors of a book about brain tumors that afflict children note:

> Parents sometimes feel that they have failed to protect their child, and they blame themselves. It is especially difficult because the cause of their child's tumor, in most instances, cannot be explained. There are questions: How could we have prevented this? What did we do wrong? How did we miss the signs? Why didn't we bring her to the doctor sooner? Why didn't we insist that the doctor do a scan? Did he inherit this from me? Why didn't we live in a safer place? Maybe I shouldn't have let her drink the well water. Was it because of the fumes from painting the house? Why? Why? Why?[4]

Anger is the next emotion patients and their families are likely to feel. Even when they recognize that no one is to blame for their brain tumor, patients may get angry at their doctors, family members, the whole world, or even some divine being. They may wonder why they were singled out to have such a serious ailment and feel angry about the unfairness of their condition.

Anger usually gives way to sadness and depression. Patients and their families grieve when they realize that their lives will never be the same—that they may never be able to fulfill their dreams and that they may be facing death. Even if their condition is not terminal, the feelings of sadness may turn into chronic depression.

Acceptance

In time, having gone through shock, denial, anger, and sadness, patients typically come to accept their condition. For some patients, acceptance may mean recognizing that their disease is terminal and that they have little time left. For other patients, acceptance may be accompanied by a sense of hope that with proper treatment their tumors will be eradicated.

One thing that helps patients and families cope is knowledge about brain tumors. Having accurate information is necessary

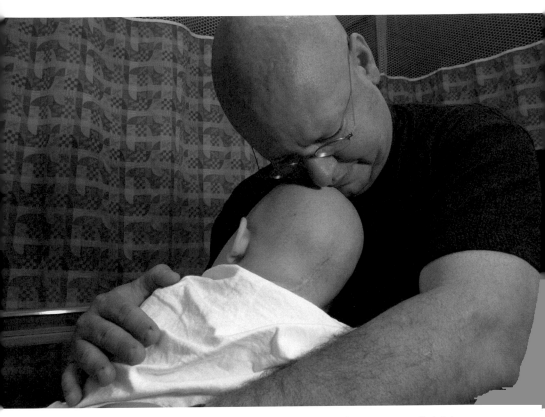

This child is being treated for a brain tumor. The parents of children with brain tumors must deal with emotions such as guilt, anger, and sadness.

for realistic expectations and planning. As difficult as the situation may be, learning the facts helps patients set aside their fears and focus on understanding the nature of their disease. Dr. Roger Cicala explains:

> Possibly no diagnosis is more frightening than a brain tumor. It is extremely important to understand, however, that a brain tumor is not just one disease; it really includes dozens of different kinds of tumors, which have very different treatments and outcomes. Certain brain tumors are among the most easily cured of all tumors while others are impossible, at present, to treat effectively.[5]

CHAPTER ONE

Understanding Brain Tumors

Tumors, which are solid masses of tissue formed by abnormal cells that grow uncontrollably, can grow anywhere in the human body, including the brain. As brain tumors grow, they irritate nearby tissues, take away nutrition and energy from healthy cells, and take up the space that would otherwise be available for normal tissue. The growth of a tumor disrupts the proper function of whatever organ it invades. Since the brain is the central governing organ in the body, any disruption in its functions poses a significant threat to the life of a brain tumor patient.

Although health professionals and others routinely use the term *brain tumor*, what is implied by the term is something more than just a tumor in the brain. As Dr. Paul Zeltzer explains, "technically speaking, many tumors in the head do not come from the brain, but rather from its coverings . . . , nerve linings . . . , glands inside the head . . . , and other tissues."[6]

To avoid confusion, some health professionals use alternate terms for brain tumors. Brain tumors are sometimes called *intracranial tumors* in reference to the cranium, or skull, in which the brain is housed. They are also referred to as *central nervous system tumors*, since the brain, along with the spinal cord, is part of the central nervous system. Most health professionals, however, use the term *brain tumor* with the understanding that it refers to tumors of all tissues inside the cranium as well as, occasionally, the spinal cord.

The term *brain tumor* may be applied to over one hundred types of abnormal masses that can form in the central nervous system. These masses may be classified according to several methods. The two broadest methods of classification separate brain tumors by their level of aggression and by their place of origin.

Malignant and Benign Tumors

In the first method of classification, brain tumors are identified as either malignant or benign based on their aggressiveness.

Even benign brain tumors, like the one shown in this color-enhanced MRI (pink area, upper right), can be dangerous.

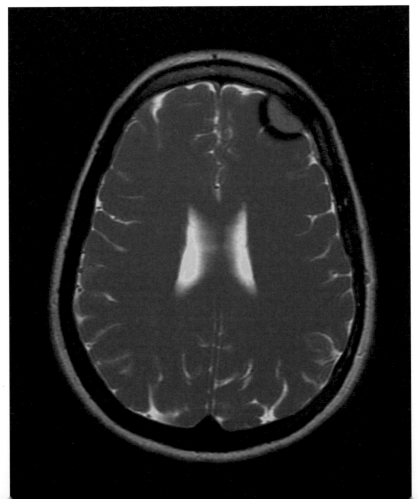

Malignant tumors contain cancerous cells that grow rapidly, infiltrate nearby tissues, and spread easily throughout the central nervous system. Benign tumors, on the other hand, grow slowly, have distinct borders, and do not infiltrate nearby tissues. To ensure uniformity in identifying the aggressiveness of a tumor, the World Health Organization has devised a system for assigning "grades" to brain tumors. In this system, tumors are assigned grades—usually expressed in Roman numerals—ranging from I to IV, with grade I being benign, or least malignant, and grade IV being the most malignant.

Experts note that classifying tumors as benign can be misleading, since even the most benign brain tumor can be danger-

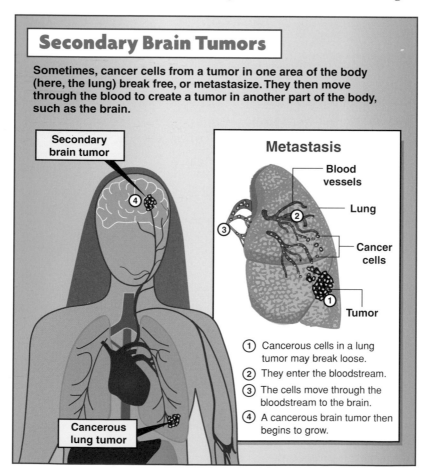

Secondary Brain Tumors

Sometimes, cancer cells from a tumor in one area of the body (here, the lung) break free, or metastasize. They then move through the blood to create a tumor in another part of the body, such as the brain.

Secondary brain tumor

Metastasis

Blood vessels

Lung

Cancer cells

Tumor

Cancerous lung tumor

(1) Cancerous cells in a lung tumor may break loose.
(2) They enter the bloodstream.
(3) The cells move through the bloodstream to the brain.
(4) A cancerous brain tumor then begins to grow.

ous if it is located in an area that controls essential bodily functions. In fact, according to Dr. Sajeel Chowdhary, depending on the location of the tumor, "a small tumor which is slow-growing can cause more grave effects than an aggressive tumor."[7] In addition, benign tumors have the potential to evolve over time into malignant tumors. Therefore, because of the brain's essential nature, and because of the potential for benign tumors to become malignant, doctors say that even benign brain tumors must be taken seriously. Dr. Chowdhary comments, "The nature of the brain often blurs the distinction between benign and malignant."[8]

Primary and Secondary Brain Tumors

Besides classifying tumors by level of aggression, doctors use a second broad method of classification based on where the brain tumor originated. In this method, brain tumors are identified as either primary or secondary tumors. Primary brain tumors, which may be benign or malignant, are masses that arise in cells in the brain. Unlike those that arise elsewhere in the body, brain tumors tend not to spread. Although primary tumors sometimes invade other sites in the brain or the spinal cord, cells from primary brain tumors do not, except in extremely rare cases, travel outside the central nervous system.

Primary brain tumors are relatively uncommon compared with secondary tumors, which form when tumor cells from other locations in the body travel to the brain. Experts refer to the travel of tumor cells from one part of the body to another as metastasis. Secondary brain tumors are therefore also known as metastatic tumors. While metastatic tumors can begin in any part of the body, the most common cancers to metastasize to the brain are malignant melanoma—a type of skin cancer—and lung and breast cancers. Because they originated elsewhere in the body, secondary brain tumors are by definition always malignant.

In addition to broad classification by level of aggression and origin, brain tumors may be more specifically classified by the type of cell in the tumor. Secondary brain tumors contain the same type of cells as the cancer from which they originated. For example, lung cancer tumors that have metastasized to the brain are known as metastasized lung tumors, even though they are located far from the lungs. Primary brain tumors, since they arise in the brain, are classified by the various types of cells found in the central nervous system.

Cells of the Central Nervous System

There are two main categories of cells in the central nervous system: neurons and glial cells, either of which can give rise to a primary brain tumor. Neurons are the cells that process information by sending electrochemical signals to other neurons via thin fibers known as axons. All thoughts, emotions, sensations, speech, movement—everything that humans think and do— are determined by these signals passing between neurons.

Glial cells, on the other hand, are not directly involved in controlling the body's function. Glial cells support neurons by surrounding them and holding them in place, by protecting them, and by supplying them with nutrients and oxygen. Glial cells outnumber neurons by at least nine to one; scientists estimate that there are 100 billion neurons and more than 900 billion glial cells in the adult human brain.

Most primary brain tumors originate in glial cells. According to the Central Brain Tumor Registry of the United States, glial cell tumors account for 42 percent of all brain tumors and 77 percent of malignant tumors. There are three types of glial cells from which tumors commonly grow: astrocytes, oligodendrocytes, and ependymal cells. Astrocytes, the most numerous glial cells, are star-shaped cells that nourish neurons and help hold them in place. Oligodendrocytes produce myelin, a membrane that surrounds and protects the axons, the thin nerve fibers of neurons. Ependymal cells line the ventricles, the four hollow chambers in the brain that are filled with cerebrospinal fluid, a clear liquid that protects and cushions the brain and spinal cord.

In addition to the neurons and glial cells of the brain itself, there are other types of cells in the central nervous system that can also give rise to tumors. These include cells of the meninges, the protective layers that cover the brain and spinal cord; the cells of the pituitary and pineal glands; and Schwann cells, which insulate and protect the nerves that connect the brain and spinal cord to sensory organs and muscles of the body.

A Confusing Naming System

The many different types of cells in which brain tumors can originate and the variation of levels of aggression make for a complex and sometimes confusing system of naming the growths. The medical name for any tumor in the body usually ends with the suffix *-oma*. For example, a tumor of Schwann cells is known as a Schwannoma, while a tumor of ependymal cells is known as an ependymoma.

This light micrograph shows star-shaped astrocytes (green), the most common glial cells. Most brain tumors consist of glial cells.

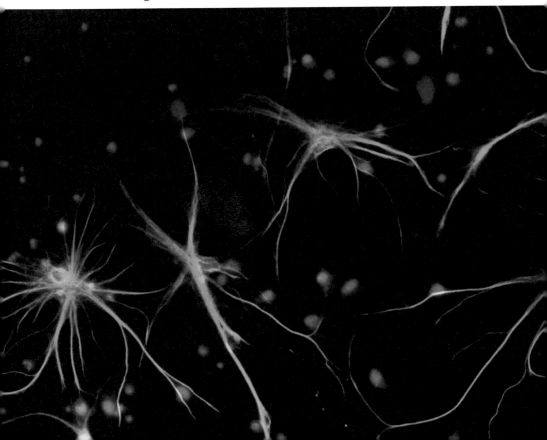

The Central Nervous System

The human nervous system consists of the central nervous system (CNS) and the peripheral nervous system (PNS). The CNS, which comprises the brain and the spinal cord, controls essential functions of the body such as heartbeat, breathing, sensation, movement, emotion, and thought. The PNS, meanwhile, includes all the nerves that carry messages back and forth from the CNS to the rest of the body. The PNS includes the cranial nerves, the twelve pairs of nerves in the brain, and the spinal nerves, the thirty-one pairs of nerves that connect the spinal cord to the body.

To protect their delicate, vital tissues, both the brain and spinal cord are immersed in a fluid known as cerebrospinal fluid. Cerebrospinal fluid is manufactured in and fills the

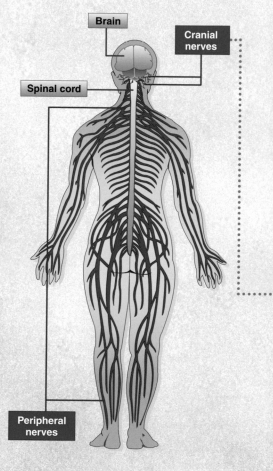

Brain

Cranial nerves

Spinal cord

Peripheral nerves

Sometimes, the same tumor is known by more than one name. For example, a tumor of glial cells is known as a glioma. However, if the glial cells involved are astrocytes, the tumor may also be known as an astrocytoma. To further complicate matters, an astrocytoma in the cerebrum, the upper part of the brain, would be known as a cerebral astrocytoma.

hollow areas of the brain known as ventricles. For further protection, the brain and spinal cord are covered by three layers of membranes known collectively as the meninges. The innermost layer of the meninges is known as the pia mater. The middle layer, a delicate tissue that resembles a spider's web, is known as the arachnoid layer. The top layer is a tough membrane known as the dura mater.

Both the brain and spinal cord are shielded by hard, bony structures. The portion of the skull that protects the brain is known as the cranium, while the spine surrounds the delicate spinal cord.

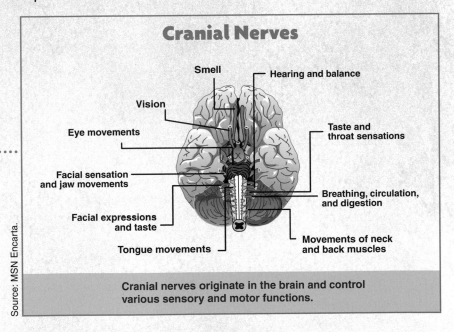

Cranial Nerves

Smell

Hearing and balance

Vision

Eye movements

Taste and throat sensations

Facial sensation and jaw movements

Breathing, circulation, and digestion

Facial expressions and taste

Tongue movements

Movements of neck and back muscles

Cranial nerves originate in the brain and control various sensory and motor functions.

Source: MSN Encarta.

If the tumor were determined to be a grade IV tumor, it would be known as a grade IV cerebral astrocytoma. More frequently, this same type of tumor is known as glioblastoma multiforme, an even more specific name that refers to the irregular shape and texture of the tumor. All of these names—glioma, astrocytoma, cerebral astrocytoma, and glioblastoma multiforme—may be used with equal validity to refer to the same tumor, although the names are progressively more specific.

This ability to refer to the same tumor with multiple names creates some confusion in the identification of brain tumors. As Dr. Paul Zeltzer comments, "There are few things more confusing to patients and caregivers than the names that are used" for brain tumors. To explain the way brain tumors are named, Zeltzer adds, "Just as a residence could be a log cabin or a brick house, a mansion or a hut, a tent in the woods or an inner-city apartment, a glioma can be further named by cell makeup, pathologic grade or location."[9]

How Brain Tumors Form

While brain tumors may be classified and identified by various systems, all tumors—whether they are malignant or benign, primary or secondary—begin when a mutation occurs in the genes of just one cell as it divides. By itself, the mutation in a single cell might not pose a problem. Some mutated cells can still perform their primary function; others are so abnormal that they simply die.

Mutations, which arise as cells multiply, are quite common. In the human body, billions of cells die and are replaced with new cells each day. To create new cells, an existing cell divides into two identical cells. All processes in cells, including division, are controlled by genes in the nucleus of each cell. One such process checks the genes of cells for damage prior to division to ensure that only healthy cells reproduce. If the cell's self-checking mechanism finds it to be healthy and normal, division proceeds. On the other hand, if the cell is abnormal, this mechanism causes it to either repair the damage or destroy itself in a form of cellular suicide. Sometimes, though, this self-check fails and the abnormal cell lives on.

When genes responsible for controlling cell division become mutated, they become known as oncogenes. Oncogenes instruct cells to divide and replicate in an uncontrolled manner. Researchers frequently compare the action of oncogenes with the action of a gas pedal stuck to the floorboard of a car. Worse still, another gene known as p53, which normally instructs an abnormal cell to stop dividing, can also mutate. When the p53 gene mutates, it fails to instruct the cell to stop dividing. In effect, a mutated p53 gene acts like a failed brake pedal in a car. Without the instruction to stop, the abnormal cell proceeds to divide into two identical, and therefore abnormal, cells. Those two abnormal cells, in turn, divide into four abnormal cells, and so on, until a mass of abnormal cells, or a tumor, is formed. Researchers say the fact that tumors result from faulty cell division explains why primary brain tumors are much more common in glial cells, which are capable of dividing, than in neurons, the vast majority of which do not divide.

How Brain Tumors Grow

Just like normal tissue, tumors, once they arise, need the steady and abundant delivery of oxygen and nutrients through blood vessels in order to survive and grow. As tumors grow, they release certain proteins into nearby tissues to stimulate angiogenesis, the formation of new blood vessels. Through angiogenesis, tumors ensure for themselves a dedicated supply of oxygen and nutrients.

Tumor cells are different from normal cells in two important ways that allow for the uncontrolled growth of abnormal masses. Normal cells typically die after fifty or sixty cycles of division. Tumor cells, however, continue to divide and replicate indefinitely. Researchers refer to this attribute of tumor cells as "immortality." Another way tumor cells differ from normal cells is that normal cells stop replicating when their outer membranes come in contact with other cells. Tumor cells, however, continue to replicate, invading adjacent tissues and allowing the tumor to grow ever larger.

What Causes Brain Tumors?

Although scientists understand how brain tumors form and grow, only in rare cases do they know what actually causes the mutation of genes that leads to brain tumors. Researchers have

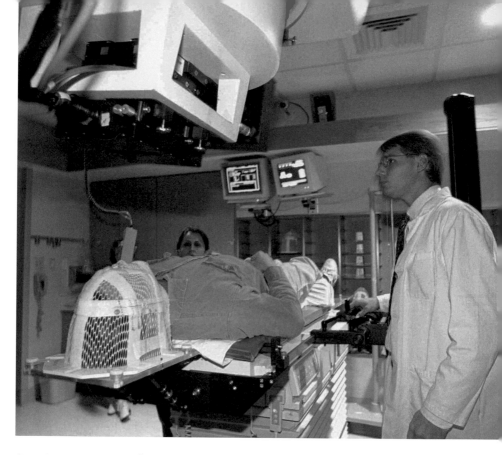

A patient receives radiation therapy for an inoperable brain tumor. Such treatments must be carefully monitored, since intense radiation may also cause cancer.

studied various environmental factors as potentially contributing to brain tumors. Of the possible causes studied, the only convincing link is exposure to powerful radiation of the sort used to treat an existing brain tumor. Other studies, focused on risk factors such as exposure to electromagnetic fields or various chemicals, have been inconclusive.

Some scientists have looked at diet as a risk factor. In animal studies, researchers have found that nitrites, which are found in cured meats, are capable of causing cancer in the nervous system. Still, researchers do not know how much exposure to nitrates might cause brain tumors in humans.

Studies have also shown that there are several viruses that can cause brain tumors in animals. Based on this evidence, researchers suspect that viruses, as well as other infectious agents and allergens, may trigger mutations in human cells and lead to cancer. No studies, though, have backed up this suspicion.

Although researchers have made little progress identifying environmental risk factors, they are more certain of the role heredity plays in making people susceptible to the mutations that lead to tumors. Simply put, this means that a general tendency to develop cancer sometimes runs in families.

In studying families of brain tumor patients, researchers have found that while only 5 percent of brain tumor patients have a relative with the same or similar illness, 19 percent of them have a relative with some other type of cancer. According to Dr. Virginia Stark-Vance, this finding "suggests that the tendency to develop genetic damage that causes abnormal cell growth may be inherited, but the tendency to develop a specific tumor may not be inherited."[10]

Prevention of Brain Tumors

With so little direct correlation between risk factors and the development of primary brain tumors, experts can only speculate as to their prevention. However, in the case of secondary brain tumors, doctors are in wide agreement. Any step that reduces the risk of developing cancer to begin with lowers the risk of developing brain tumors. Metastasized lung tumors are an example. Dr. Stark-Vance explains:

> Cigarette smoking has not been clearly associated with an increased risk for the development of primary brain tumors, but cigarette smoking is an important cause of metastatic brain tumors, particularly those that originate

from lung cancer. Of the 170,000 lung cancer patients diagnosed each year in the United States, about one third will develop one or more tumors in the brain—more than 55,000
people![11]

The Human Brain

The brain consists of four main parts: the brain stem, the cerebellum,
the diencephalon, and the cerebrum. At the base of the brain, joining
the brain to the spinal cord, is the brain stem. It controls vital functions such as heartbeat and breathing. The brain stem is also where
most of the cranial nerves, such as the hearing, taste, and facial
nerves, begin. The cerebellum, located just behind the brain stem, is
responsible for movement, balance, and posture.

The diencephalon is found in the core of the brain, above the brain
stem. The diencephalon contains the thalamus, the hypothalamus,
the pituitary gland, and the pineal gland. The thalamus is involved in

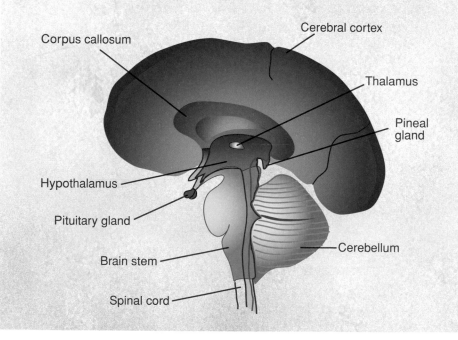

The idea that reducing the incidence of tumors elsewhere in the body would cut the number of new cases of brain tumors is borne out by statistics. According to the American Brain Tumor Association, of the 190,000 patients diagnosed with brain

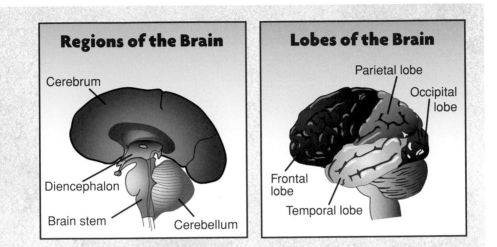

Regions of the Brain

Cerebrum

Diencephalon

Brain stem   Cerebellum

Lobes of the Brain

Parietal lobe

Occipital lobe

Frontal lobe

Temporal lobe

the relay of information from the sensory organs to the brain, while the hypothalamus is responsible for regulating appetite, thirst, and the body's response to anxiety. Attached to the hypothalamus is the pituitary gland, which directs the production of hormones such as those that regulate growth, metabolism, and puberty. Also at the core of the brain is the pineal gland, which is involved in the regulation of daily sleep/wake cycles and temperature.

The cerebrum, the largest area of the brain, controls thought, judgment, perception, language, imagination, and voluntary movement. Its outer layer, known as the cerebral cortex, is divided into two sections: the left and right hemispheres. The right hemisphere controls the left side of the body, while the left hemisphere controls the right side of the body. Each hemisphere is divided into four sections, known as lobes. The frontal lobe controls some speech production, movement, emotions, and reasoning. The parietal lobe controls sensations of touch, pain, and temperature. The temporal lobe controls hearing, aspects of speech not controlled by the frontal lobe, and memory. The occipital lobe, also known as the visual cortex, controls vision.

tumors each year in the United States, more than three-quarters (150,000) have metastatic brain tumors. In theory, at least, these tumors would not have occurred if the original cancers could have been prevented.

In any case, preventing primary brain tumors would have relatively little impact on overall cancer rates in the United States. The Central Brain Tumor Registry of the United States, which keeps track of primary brain tumors only, estimated in its 2004–2005 report that 41,130 Americans, including 3,200 children and teenagers, would be diagnosed with primary brain tumors in 2004. Of those expected to develop primary brain tumors, slightly more than half are expected to have malignancies.

Who Gets Brain Tumors?

Primary malignant brain tumors, then, are rare compared with other cancers. They account for less than 2 percent of all cancers in adults. In children and teenagers, however, the story is different. Brain tumors are the most common of the solid tumors among children and teens, accounting for 20 percent of all cancers in these age groups. Brain tumors are also the leading cause of death from solid tumors in children and teenagers.

Although brain tumors are rare, a slight but steady rise in their incidence, particularly among the elderly, has been reported in the last twenty years. Doctors believe that the rise is due partly to improved diagnostic methods and partly to increased life expectancy. Another factor that contributes to the rise in brain tumor incidence is that in recent years, with improved treatment methods, more patients of other cancers have survived, creating a larger group of people likely to develop metastatic tumors of the brain.

Although brain tumors affect both adults and youngsters, there are differences in the location of tumors in each age group. Adults are more likely to have tumors in the cerebrum, the upper part of the brain, while children are more likely to have tumors in the cerebellum and the brain stem, which are located in the back and bottom areas of the brain. Some types of tumors predominantly affect adults, while others are more common among children. For example, adults are much more likely than children to have metastatic tumors since adults, having lived longer, are more likely to have had other cancers that metastasize to the brain.

Regardless of their age, patients with brain tumors begin to experience unsettling effects as their tumors grow. While tumors in any part of the body are undesirable, what makes brain tumors especially problematic is the essential nature of the brain's functions. The brain controls vital functions such as heartbeat, breathing, all sensations, movement, thoughts, and emotions. When tumors disrupt any of these critical functions, the patient's well-being is placed in jeopardy. According to Dr. Roger Cicala, "People can have significant damage to their heart, liver, kidneys, or other organs and still live fairly normal lives. Even minor damage to the brain, however, significantly interferes with a person's ability to function and perform even the simplest everyday tasks."[12] The symptoms caused by brain tumors may at first be subtle and mild. In time, however, they become sufficiently noticeable that those suffering from the symptoms seek medical help.

CHAPTER TWO

Diagnosis of Brain Tumors

Since the brain is ultimately responsible for all behavior, thought, and bodily function, tumors in this essential organ cause a wide range of symptoms. Until the late nineteenth century, doctors frequently considered these symptoms to be diseases in themselves and did not realize that they were caused by brain tumors. The diagnosis of brain tumors was especially difficult because masses in the brain, shielded by the hard, bony skull, could not be detected by plain observation. With the advent of modern diagnostic procedures and tools, however, doctors became able to accurately detect and diagnose brain tumors.

The most common symptoms that afflict patients with brain tumors occur when the mass grows large enough to put pressure on nearby tissues. Since the cranium cannot stretch to make room for the growing tumor, tissues adjacent to the tumor are squeezed and compressed. The compression in turn causes the tissues to swell, further increasing the level of what experts refer to as intracranial pressure. Moreover, some tumors also block the flow of cerebrospinal fluid, the protective liquid that surrounds both the brain and the spinal cord. This blockage causes intracranial pressure to rise further still. This rise in intracranial pressure—whether resulting from the mass itself, the irritated nearby tissues, or the blocked cerebrospinal fluid—is responsible for the most common symptoms of brain tumors: headaches that do not respond to medication, nausea and vomiting, and seizures.

Headaches

It is estimated that 60 to 70 percent of patients with brain tumors suffer from headaches. Far more severe and continuous than headaches caused by tension, these are what prompt

A large brain tumor (blue) is clearly visible in this scan. Large tumors increase intracranial pressure, which leads to headaches, vomiting, and seizures.

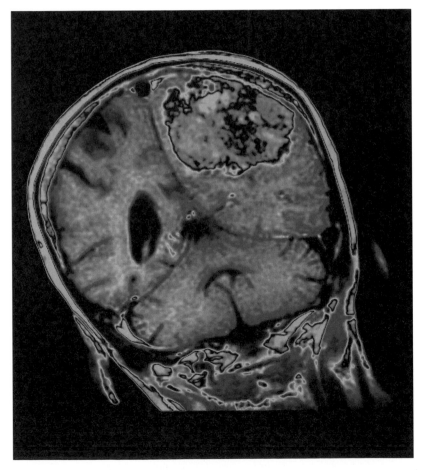

A severe headache does not necessarily indicate a brain tumor.

more than half of patients to first seek medical help. These headaches differ from ordinary ones in that they are usually worse in the morning. This is because pressure in the brain increases when the sufferer lies down. Headaches may also occur when patients bend or exercise because the shift in position may cause intracranial pressure to change suddenly.

Doctors say that the headache pain does not originate in the brain tissues, since the brain itself is not sensitive to pain. As Dr. David van Alstine comments, "[The brain] can even be operated on while a patient is entirely awake, as long as the scalp and the overlying tissues are anesthetized with a local anesthetic."[13] What brain tumor patients experience as headaches results from the swollen brain tissues pushing against the meninges, the brain's protective membranes, which are sensitive to pain.

Headaches by themselves, of course, are not necessarily symptoms of brain tumors. Although they are common among brain tumor patients, headaches also affect millions of otherwise healthy people. Therefore, a doctor who examines a patient with a headache is not likely to suspect a tumor unless the patient also has other symptoms associated with brain tumors.

Some doctors say that the patient's age should be considered when deciding whether a brain tumor might be present. These doctors note that while headaches are common in adults, headaches in children are rare and should be viewed with suspicion. According to Dr. Virginia Stark-Vance, "More than 99% of adults who suffer from headache do not have a brain tumor." She goes on to suggest that since "children seem to suffer headaches less frequently than adults, a child who complains of headache should always raise the suspicion of a brain tumor."[14]

Nausea and Vomiting

In addition to headaches, increased intracranial pressure may also cause nausea and vomiting. The sensation of nausea and the subsequent vomiting are among the body's many involuntary actions controlled by the brain stem. Like headaches, nausea and vomiting are common among brain tumor patients, but they also occur in people with other, much more common illnesses such as digestive disorders, stomach flu, or food poisoning. Therefore, patients as well as doctors may not realize that a patient's nausea is caused by a brain tumor unless the patient also suffers from other symptoms such as headaches and seizures.

Seizures

The term *seizure* refers to a brief, sudden, and involuntary spasm of muscles as well as episodes of unconsciousness.

Seizures occur when for some reason the neurons' normal process of transferring electrical charges is disrupted by intense bursts of electrical energy. A simple way to explain seizures would be to say that "seizures can be compared to an electrical storm in the brain."[15]

Like other symptoms associated with brain tumors, most seizures are caused by other conditions. When a patient goes to a doctor after experiencing a seizure, the physician will probably order a series of tests to eliminate other possible explanations, such as epilepsy.

Seizures may be either partial or generalized. As the term implies, partial seizures affect only one area of the brain. For example, a partial seizure may cause one of the patient's hands to suddenly jerk and twitch. Generalized seizures, on the other hand, affect the whole body. In a generalized seizure, the patient may have spasms in the arms, legs, or trunk; may have trouble breathing; and may briefly lose consciousness. Either generalized or partial seizures can result from a brain tumor.

Not every brain tumor causes seizures, however. Experts estimate that one-third of brain tumor patients experience seizures. The location of a tumor seems to be a factor. Masses in any part of the brain may cause seizures, but they are most likely to occur when tumors are in the cerebrum, the part of the brain responsible for thought and conscious movement.

Other Effects

In addition to headaches, nausea, and seizures, brain tumor patients may have other symptoms that are more specifically related to the location of the tumor. For example, a tumor in the cerebellum, the portion of the brain that is responsible for coordination, may cause the patient to have difficulty with posture, balance, and walking. A tumor in the pituitary gland, which controls the production of hormones, including growth hormone, may cause abnormal enlargement of a patient's hands and feet. Other symptoms of brain tumors include weakness or numbness in the legs or arms; difficulty with speech, writing, or reading; sensory disturbances such as double vision, ringing in the ear, or experiencing unusual scents and tastes; memory loss and difficulties with attention; and personality changes.

The location of a tumor may also determine the severity of the symptom. Depending on its location, even a small tumor may cause unbearable and persistent symptoms. Conversely, a large tumor may cause very mild and subtle effects. Dr. Roger Cicala writes:

> For example, a tumor one centimeter (about 1/3 inch) in diameter located in the brain stem will almost always cause significant

A brain tumor's symptoms are determined by its location. Even a tiny tumor in a vital area like the brain stem can cause crippling symptoms.

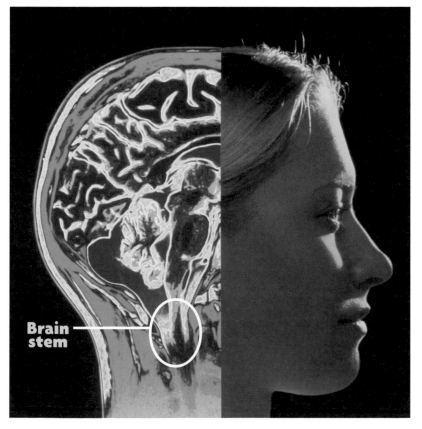

Brain stem

symptoms. On the other hand, a meningioma (tumor of the brain's covering tissue) located over the frontal lobes may grow to be several inches in diameter while causing only vague symptoms such as headache or forgetfulness.[16]

Whatever the symptoms, whether mild or severe, doctors may at first suspect other conditions, especially since brain tumors are relatively rare. For example, an elderly patient who complains of forgetfulness may initially be diagnosed as suffering from dementia when the real cause of memory loss is a tumor in the temporal lobe of the cerebrum. It may take some time before doctors rule out other diseases and begin to suspect that a patient's symptoms are caused by a brain tumor.

Historical Diagnosis of Symptoms

Once more likely causes of a patient's symptoms have been eliminated, a doctor can usually pinpoint the type and location of a tumor. This ability is relatively recent. Not until the late nineteenth century did doctors know enough

Scientist Paul Broca identified a part of the brain that controls speech. This and similar discoveries made it possible to locate brain tumors based on symptoms.

about the brain to understand how a tumor could produce symptoms. Indeed, for millennia symptoms such as headaches, nausea, and seizures were seen as diseases in themselves, and doctors did their best to alleviate them, never realizing they were caused by tumors in the brain.

Despite advances in the understanding of human anatomy beginning in the sixteenth century, the diagnosis of brain tumors remained nearly impossible because doctors could not actually examine their patients' brains without causing severe or fatal injury.

Only in the nineteenth century, with the discovery of anesthesia, was surgery of any kind really practical. Furthermore, until Joseph Lister's work in developing antiseptic or sterile measures for hospital procedures became widely known, survival following surgery was nothing but sheer luck, especially when the brain was involved. According to historian of neuroscience Stanley Finger, "Prior to Lister, the [act] of opening the skull, cutting the meninges, and exposing the brain to the elements was a virtual death sentence."[17]

Anesthesia and antiseptic measures, though highly important, were not sufficient to ensure the accurate diagnosis of brain tumors. Even when doctors suspected that a patient had a brain tumor, they had no way to determine the location of the tumor without causing massive brain damage. What made it possible for doctors to determine the location of a tumor was the discovery, made by several scientists in the mid-1800s, that specific areas of the cerebral cortex correlated to specific functions of the brain. For example, scientists Paul Broca and Carl Wernicke identified areas in the cerebral cortex that were related to the understanding and production of speech. The acceptance in the scientific community of this concept, known as cortical localization, paved the way for physicians to link symptoms of brain tumors to specific locations in the brain. As Stanley Finger explains:

> For the first time, surgeons were able to localize where tumors, infections, and foreign objects were most likely to be found

solely on the basis of symptoms, such as a paralysis of one of the body parts, or problems recognizing sounds. This advance was especially important when there were no clues on the skull to suggest the location of a tumor, an abscess, or a comparable problem.[18]

In 1879, Scottish surgeon William Macewan, who was a follower of both Broca and Lister, achieved an enormous advance, not just in diagnosis, but in treatment of a brain tumor. Macewan's patient was a teenager who exhibited seizures and twitching of the arm and face. Macewan thought that these symptoms indicated a tumor in the motor region of the patient's cerebral cortex. He removed the tumor, and the patient lived for eight more years.

Another significant discovery—one that would form the basis of modern diagnostic techniques—occurred in 1895, when German scientist William Roentgen discovered X-rays. Roentgen's discovery made it possible for doctors to see the inside of the body without having to cut it open. Although details of soft tissues such as the brain are not clearly visible in simple X-rays, refined techniques and tools eventually allowed doctors to detect brain tumors without needing to open the patient's skull.

Modern Diagnosis of Brain Tumors

While sophisticated imaging tools make the diagnosis of brain tumors easier, doctors continue to rely on their knowledge of the brain's anatomy and the functioning of its many intricate structures to home in on where a tumor might lie. Because of the specialized knowledge required, this task usually falls to a neurologist or possibly a neurosurgeon. The specialist tests the patient's reflexes, sensations such as vision and hearing, balance, movement, memory, and thought processes. Eventually, according to Dr. Cicala, "By carefully determining the areas of brain function that aren't working properly, a good neurologist or neurosurgeon can usually tell exactly where (to within fractions of an inch) a problem in the brain is located."[19] If the neu-

Caring for Brain Tumor Patients: It's a Team Effort

In the course of diagnosis and treatment, patients with brain tumors receive care from many specially trained physicians. These physicians work together as a team to ensure accurate diagnosis and appropriate treatment for brain tumor patients.

Neurologist: A neurologist is a medical doctor who specializes in the diagnosis and treatment of disorders and diseases of the brain.

Neuro-oncologist: An oncologist is a medical doctor who specializes in the diagnosis and treatment of cancer. A neuro-oncologist is an oncologist who has received further training in cancers of the nervous system.

Neuropathologist: A pathologist is a medical doctor who is trained to examine and evaluate cells and tissues for the presence of disease. A neuropathologist is a pathologist who specializes in analyzing cells and tissues of the nervous system, including cells from brain tumors.

Neuroradiologist: A radiologist is a medical doctor who is trained to interpret a variety of diagnostic images, including X-rays, CT scans, PET scans, and MRI scans. A neuroradiologist is trained specifically to view images related to the nervous system.

Neurosurgeon: A neurosurgeon is a surgeon who specializes in surgery of the central nervous system. Neurosurgeons also perform biopsies, surgical procedures in which tumor cells are extracted to be analyzed by a neuropathologist.

Radiation oncologist: A radiation oncologist is a physician with special training and experience in treating tumors by radiation.

rologist suspects a brain tumor, the patient is usually referred to a hospital or a medical center for more detailed testing. Here a wide variety of personnel—including neurologists, neurosurgeons, pathologists, oncologists, radiologists, and imaging technicians—typically get involved in the diagnostic process.

Imaging Tests

The primary diagnostic tools these specialists rely on are imaging tests. Radiologists use several imaging techniques to determine the presence and exact location of tumors inside the brain. The most commonly used imaging tests are computed axial tomography (CAT or CT), magnetic resonance imaging (MRI), and positron emission tomography (PET). All these imaging techniques were developed in the 1970s and 1980s.

CT combines the use of traditional X-rays and computer processing to produce images of tissues in the brain. During a CT scan, the patient lies on a table that moves slowly through a doughnut-shaped machine. As the table moves forward, a small X-ray tube rotates around the patient's head, taking hundreds of cross-sectional images, often called "slices," of the brain. The images may be viewed individually, or they may be combined through computer processing into a single three-dimensional image.

Unlike CT scans, MRIs do not use X-rays or other forms of radiation. MRIs use a powerful magnetic field to produce images. During an MRI, the patient lies on a table that slides into an enclosed cylinder. A powerful magnet causes individual molecules within cells to vibrate or resonate. A computer then interprets these vibrations to produce detailed, three-dimensional images of the brain's tissues.

Although both CTs and MRIs may be used to detect brain tumors, doctors generally prefer MRIs because the images are more detailed. The equipment needed to conduct MRIs is much more expensive than CT equipment, however, so not all medical centers offer such tests. Furthermore, implanted medical devices such as heart pacemakers can be damaged by the intense magnetism during an MRI.

CT and MRI scans indicate the location, size, and shape of tumors. PET scans, on the other hand, allow doctors to determine how aggressive a tumor is. PET scans are occasionally used after a tumor has already been detected by a CT or MRI scan. In PET scans, a special radioactive substance is injected into the brain. The substance is usually a form of sugar or pro-

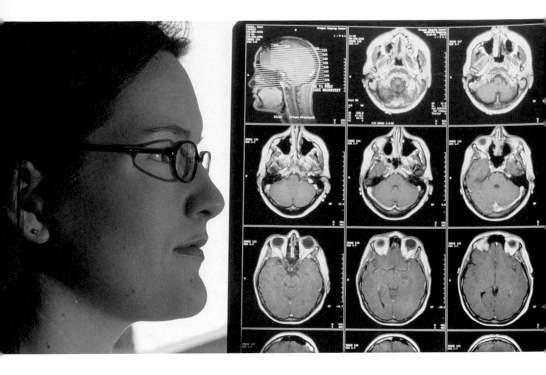

This brain cancer patient received successful experimental therapy. In this photo, she poses next to a scan showing no signs of cancer.

tein that is known to be used by brain tumors for energy. Once the radioactive substance is injected, the PET scan can indicate the rate of its absorption by the tumor. The higher the rate of absorption, the more aggressive the cancer is likely to be. Doctors generally need to determine the aggression level of the tumor in order to decide on the most appropriate treatment.

Occasionally, in addition to CT, MRI, and PET scans, doctors order an angiogram, which is a special X-ray that highlights blood vessels. This tests helps doctors identify the blood vessels that are supplying nourishment to a tumor.

Biopsy

Although imaging scans clearly show the location of abnormal masses, doctors cannot know for certain that an abnormal mass is a tumor based on imaging scans alone. Sometimes, for example, an injury or a lesion such as a cyst or abscess may also appear as an abnormal mass in imaging scans. According

Waiting to Hear the News

In the book The Human Side of Cancer, *psychiatrist Jimmie C. Holland writes about the emotional upheaval that patients undergo as they wait for test results:*

Many people's first experience with cancer begins quite simply with the discovery of symptom or sign known to be a possible cancer indicator. . . . From this moment, the uncertainty of cancer begins. Could this symptom mean cancer, or can I assume it's nothing?

But this moment, before the doctor has even been called or a single test has been done, often transforms a person's life from one of general well-being to one of enormous anxiety and uncertainty about the future. This pervasive sense of uncertainty probably characterizes the journey with cancer more than anything else. . . . This seems to be what people mean when they say, "The diagnosis completely changed my life." . . .

Once you have seen the doctor and had an examination, and the tests have been ordered—such as a biopsy, scans . . . —your thoughts may alternate between "It's probably nothing" and "I know it's the worst." Feelings of optimism and despair change from hour to hour. This is part of the response to the possibility of hearing bad news: anticipating what you may feel should it be cancer. Many people share with me that this is one of the most difficult times for them—waiting to hear the news.

Waiting to learn the results of lab tests can be agonizing.

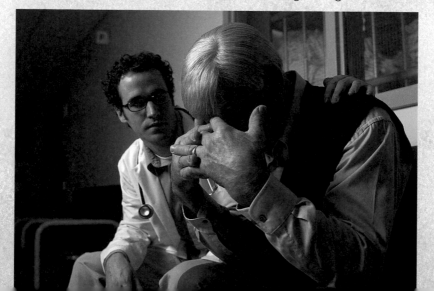

to Dr. Stark-Vance, "The only way to determine whether that abnormality is a tumor is by examination of a sample of the abnormality under the microscope."[20] In a diagnostic procedure known as a biopsy, a neurosurgeon removes a small sample of tissue from the suspected tumor to be examined under a microscope by a pathologist.

There are two types of biopsies: open and closed biopsies. In an open biopsy, a neurosurgeon cuts through the scalp, removes a small portion of the skull, and cuts through the meninges and the necessary portion of the brain to reach the suspected tumor. A small sample of the mass is then removed to be examined by a neuropathologist. Almost always, since the skull has been opened and the brain exposed, the neurosurgeon proceeds to remove all or part of the tumor, even before the pathology report comes in. Sometimes, of course, an open biopsy is not appropriate. In cases where the tumor may be difficult to reach, for example, the neurosurgeon may choose to perform a closed biopsy. In this procedure, a small hole is made in the scalp and skull, and a thin needle is inserted through the hole into the location indicated by the imaging scans. The surgeon then uses the needle to suck up a small sample of the tumor to be examined under a microscope.

Biopsy Alternative

While a biopsy is the most reliable method of confirming the presence of a brain tumor, it may not always be possible. When tumors are located in critical areas of the brain, the risk of injury from the biopsy may be too large. For example, a biopsy of a mass in the brain stem is often impossible because the brain stem controls essential functions such as breathing and heartbeat.

Occasionally, if a direct biopsy of the brain tissue is not possible, doctors perform a procedure known as lumbar puncture, or spinal tap. In this procedure, a sample of cerebrospinal fluid is drawn from the spine to be checked for tumor cells. These procedures, however, are useful only for diagnosing cancers that shed cells into the cerebrospinal fluid.

Once the sample tissue has been removed by either open or closed biopsy, a neuropathologist examines the tissue under a microscope. The neuropathologist determines what type of cells the tumor has and how aggressive it is. The grading of a tumor's aggressiveness is a tricky task, complicated by the fact that a tumor may contain several types of cells displaying a range of malignancy. In such a case, the pathologist assigns the grade of the most malignant cells in the sample. As Dr. Cicala explains, this approach makes sense "because over time the highest grade (and therefore most rapidly growing) cells will become the most common type of cell in the tumor."[21]

Identifying the cell type and grade of a tumor is an essential preliminary of determining its appropriate treatment. For some low-grade tumors, such as benign meningiomas, surgery to remove the tumor may be the only treatment the doctor recommends. For tumors that are high-grade, large, or located in especially hard-to-reach and critical areas of the brain, surgery may not be possible or it may need to be followed by other therapies. Occasionally, doctors choose to observe very small, slow-growing tumors while managing symptoms such as headaches, nausea, and seizures with medication. According to Dr. Sajeel Chowdhary, once the pathologist has determined the exact type of tumor, it is up to the medical team then to "tailor the therapy to every patient."[22] Therapy, then, is an art in itself.

CHAPTER THREE

Treatment of Brain Tumors

Once the presence of a brain tumor has been confirmed, doctors aim to remove it altogether or shrink it as much as possible while preserving the brain's functions. To accomplish this goal, doctors have three approaches available: surgery, radiotherapy, and chemotherapy. These forms of treatment are sometimes used alone, but they are typically used in combination with one another. In addition, various medications may be necessary—to treat the symptoms caused by the tumor and to prevent or minimize any side effects from the treatment.

Surgery

In treating brain tumors, surgery is almost always the first option to be considered because it is the most direct method of getting rid of the tumor. Surgeons use the term *resection* to refer to the removal of tissue anywhere in the body. In resecting brain tumors, neurosurgeons aim for "gross total resection," or complete removal of the tumor, because even one cancerous cell, if left behind, can potentially multiply and form a new mass. Furthermore, removal of the entire tumor is most likely to alleviate the patient's symptoms. As Dr. Sajeel Chowdhary comments, "The more extensive the tumor resection, the better the prognosis."[23]

The problem, of course, is that oftentimes the tumor has infiltrated nearby tissues, making a gross total resection impractical.

Dr. Neil Feldstein cites an analogy frequently used to describe the neurosurgeon's task:

> To use a food analogy, tumors in the brain are more like a pat of butter on toast. The same way that melted butter spreads into all the little nooks, brain tumors "infiltrate" into normal surrounding brain tissue. The only way to remove all of the butter would be to cut out some of the bread. Similarly, the only way to remove all of the viable tumor is to remove some normal tissue. . . . [T]he extent of infiltration and the location of the tumor would help determine the degree to which the tumor could be safely removed.[24]

In removing brain tumors, then, neurosurgeons must balance the need to preserve vital brain structures that are located near the tumor against the desirability of removing all the cancerous cells. According to Dr. Paul Zeltzer, "Even though the goal of surgery is to remove the tumor, the first priority is to preserve . . . neurological function. When total removal of the tumor carries significant risk of *morbidity* (any side effect that can decrease quality of life), it's better to leave some tumor behind."[25] If a neurosurgeon determines that total resection is not safe, then the tumor is partially reduced in a procedure known as debulking.

Once the neurosurgeon decides that total or partial removal of a tumor is possible, the operation, known as a craniotomy, can proceed. The neurosurgeon determines the point on the skull that offers the best access to the tumor while avoiding vital brain structures. Once the patient has been anesthetized and the scalp shaved and scrubbed, the neurosurgeon cuts through the scalp to expose the skull. A portion of the skull is then removed and placed aside in a sterile salt solution. The meninges, the outer protective layers of the brain, are next cut to expose the outer surface of the brain itself. The neurosurgeon then cuts through the brain tissues and removes as much of the tumor as possible. The open space left by the removal of the tumor is then filled with sterile salt solution. The cut in the

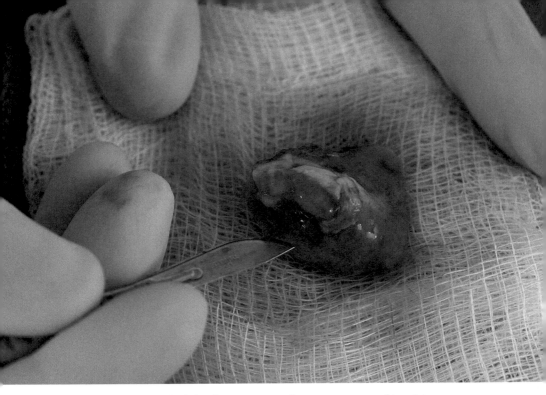

A pathologist holds a brain tumor that was removed in a biopsy. Surgery is frequently the first course of action against brain cancer.

meninges is sutured, the piece of skull previously removed is replaced, and the scalp incision is sutured.

Especially when a tumor is located near or in the cerebrum, the neurosurgeon's job is complicated by the need to determine the precise functions of what are known as "eloquent" areas. These are the areas of the cerebral cortex responsible for producing and understanding speech, originating voluntary movement, and interpreting sensations. Although these functions are located in the same parts of the brain in all people, individual variability means that the neurosurgeon needs to determine with great precision the function of a particular area of the brain in each patient. The procedure for determining which specific locations of the brain relate to which functions is known as brain mapping.

To map a patient's brain, the neurosurgeon awakens the patient after the skull is opened and the brain is exposed. This is possible because only the scalp, skull, and meninges feel pain—the brain itself has no pain sensors. Once the patient is

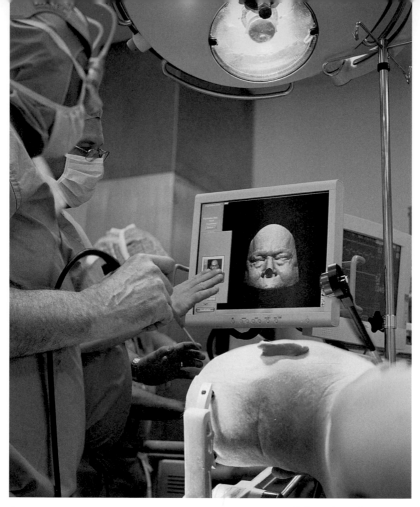

Surgeons use a computer to map a cancer patient's head so they can avoid harming vital areas of the brain when they operate.

awake the neurosurgeon uses a probe that delivers a very low electrical current to stimulate the areas in question in order to determine their function. For example, the surgeon will probe an area while the patient speaks. If the patient is suddenly unable to speak, the surgeon identifies that particular spot as an eloquent area that must be avoided during the surgery. After the brain mapping is completed, the patient receives anesthesia once more and the surgery continues.

Radiotherapy

For some fortunate patients, surgery is the only necessary treatment. Most, however, especially those with malignant, infiltrating tumors, require radiotherapy following surgery to destroy those cancerous tissues that the surgery could not eliminate. Even in cases where the tumor has been completely removed surgically, radiotherapy is often recommended just to make sure that any stray tumor cells near the tumor site are destroyed. Sometimes, when the tumor is in an inaccessible area

Supplementary and Alternative Surgical Procedures

While craniotomies are the most common surgical procedure for brain tumors, some patients may need additional or alternative procedures. One of these procedures, known as shunt implantation, is used to relieve intracranial pressure. In some patients, brain tumors block the normal flow of the cerebrospinal fluid. This blockage causes an increase in cerebrospinal fluid that in turn causes an increase in intracranial pressure. To drain the excess fluid, neurosurgeons implant in the brain a tube known as a shunt. Shunts drain the fluid from the brain either into a collection bag outside the body or into the abdominal cavity, where the fluid is absorbed. Shunts are usually implanted before tumor surgery and then removed. Sometimes, however, shunts may be needed, either temporarily or permanently, to continue draining excess fluid even after removal of the tumor.

While shunts are implanted in preparation for craniotomies, another procedure, known as transsphenoidal surgery, may be performed as an alternative to craniotomy. Transsphenoidal surgery is typically used to remove pituitary tumors. In this procedure, surgeons make an incision in the sphenoid sinus area behind the nose and upper lip without disturbing the rest of the skull. The incision gives the surgeon access to the pituitary gland, which is located behind the sphenoid sinus.

of the brain such as the brain stem, radiotherapy is used instead of surgery.

Radiotherapy works by damaging tumor cells so that they can no longer divide and replicate. In order to damage cells, high-energy rays, which are produced by equipment known as linear accelerators, are beamed to the patient's tumor. These therapeutic rays are much more powerful than X-rays used for routine diagnostic tests. According to Dr. Myles Lampenfeld, a radiation oncologist, "While low-energy X rays (like routine chest X rays or dental films) can harmlessly pass through the body, creating a photographic image, the high-energy X rays directed to the tumor damage the cells they come in contact with."[26]

Although radiation therapy will destroy a tumor, there is a problem in that it can also damage normal tissue. Moreover, the effects are cumulative: They build up with repeated doses. If a patient receives too many doses, brain damage results.

To avoid this sort of damage from radiation, patients may receive what is known as intensity modulated radiation therapy (IMRT). The American Brain Tumor Association says that the IMRT method makes use of CT scans and computers to shape radiation beams to conform to "the size, shape and location of a tumor, matching the radiation dose to the contour of the tumor while minimizing the impact on surrounding healthy tissue."[27] Since the beams are adjusted to conform to the tumors, IMRT can be used to treat tumors of any size and may be used for multiple tumors.

Another advantage of IMRT is that it can be used for patients who have already received the maximum dose of radiation through conventional radiotherapy. For patients whose tumors do not respond to the maximum dosage, or for patients whose tumors recur, IMRT allows them to receive additional radiation that may alleviate their symptoms and prolong their lives.

Stereotactic Radiosurgery

While conventional radiotherapy and IMRT require a series of treatments, another form of radiotherapy known as stereotactic radiosurgery is used in a single session in which a very high dose of precise and focused radiation is beamed to the brain tumor. Despite the implication of the term, radiosurgery does not involve any physical cutting of tissue. According to the International RadioSurgery Association (IRSA), "Radiosurgery . . . has such a dramatic effect in the target zone that the changes are considered 'surgical.'"[28]

An instrument known as the Gamma Knife, which uses gamma rays from radioactive cobalt to destroy tumor cells, is widely used for radiosurgery. The IRSA describes how the Gamma Knife works as follows:

> Gamma Knife surgery is unique in that no surgical incision is made to expose the inside of the brain, thereby reducing the risk of surgical complications and eliminating the side effects and dangers of general anesthesia. The "Blades" of the Gamma Knife are the beams of gamma radiation programmed to target the lesion at the point where they intersect. In a single treatment

This patient is receiving a precise radiation treatment called stereotactic radiosurgery, which is an alternative to open-brain surgery.

session, 201 beams of gamma radiation focus precisely on the lesion. Over time, most lesions slowly decrease in size and dissolve. The exposure is brief and only the tissue being treated receives a significant radiation dose, while the surrounding tissue remains unharmed.[29]

Stereotactic radiosurgery may be used in place of surgery or in combination with more conventional surgery. It may also be used following conventional radiotherapy or IMRT. Radiosurgery, however, cannot be used to treat large tumors since it is so narrowly focused. It is most useful in treating single, small tumors that have not infiltrated healthy adjacent tissues.

Brachytherapy

While radiosurgery differs from both conventional radiotherapy and IMRT, all three forms of radiotherapy may be classified as external radiotherapies. That is to say, radiation beams from equipment such as a linear accelerator or a Gamma Knife are directed at a tumor from outside the patient's body. By contrast, internal radiotherapy, also known as brachytherapy, employs a source of radiation that is placed inside the patient's body.

Brachytherapy involves the implantation of small, rice-shaped pellets containing radioactive iodine or another chemical element near the site of the tumor. These pellets deliver continuous but low doses of radiation directly into the tumor. Brachytherapy is especially useful for patients with tumors that cannot be completely removed because surgery risks damaging critical areas of the brain. Brachytherapy may also be used following conventional radiotherapy in order to kill off remaining cancer cells without causing brain damage.

Chemotherapy

For many brain tumor patients, surgery and one or more forms of radiotherapy are sufficient to eradicate tumors. For patients whose tumors fail to respond to those treatments, chemotherapy is the only remaining hope. Chemotherapy is also used in combination with radiotherapy in cases where surgery is not an option.

Chemotherapy is the administration of anticancer drugs to disrupt the growth of tumors. These drugs may be given to patients by mouth, injected into a vein, or injected into a muscle. Regardless of the method, the chemotherapy drug eventually enters the patient's bloodstream to be carried to the tumor site. Chemotherapy, unlike surgery and radiotherapy, is therefore known as a "systemic" treatment, since the patient's entire body or system is affected as the drugs course through the bloodstream.

There are two major categories of chemotherapy drugs. The first category of drugs, known as "cytotoxic" drugs, destroys existing tumor cells. The second category, known as "cytostatic" drugs, attempts to disrupt the tumor cells' ability to divide and replicate. Within these two categories are dozens of drugs that work in slightly different ways. While these drugs may be used singly, they are often much more effective when used in combination with one another. According to Dr. Cicala, "Administering small doses of several drugs—each of which damages tumor cells in a different way—can be much more effective than a high dose of a single drug."[30] Because of the wide range of anticancer drugs, doctors may need to experiment in order to find the protocol—that is, the drug or combination of drugs, the dosage, and the timing of doses—that best suits an individual patient's needs.

Blood-Brain Barrier

One difficulty with chemotherapy for brain tumors is a phenomenon known as the blood-brain barrier. The blood vessels serving most of the brain are lined with special cells that let oxygen and nutrients enter brain tissues but keep out large molecules—which, unfortunately, exactly describes many chemotherapy agents. To get around the barrier, patients are given a drug that temporarily inactivates the blood-brain barrier and allows the chemotherapy drugs to pass through to brain tissues. Such drugs cannot be used for long, however, since doing so would leave the brain vulnerable to infections as well as disrupt the production of certain vital hormones.

Another method of overcoming the blood-brain barrier is a reservoir and pump system known as the Ommaya Reservoir.

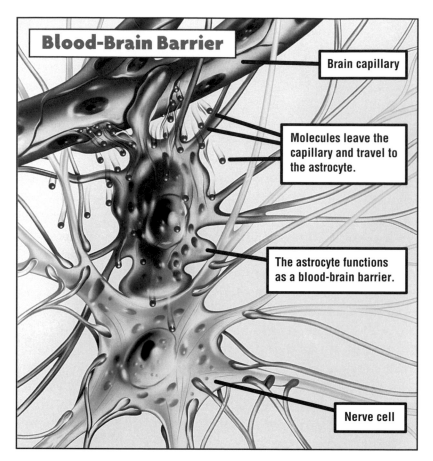

Blood-Brain Barrier

Brain capillary

Molecules leave the capillary and travel to the astrocyte.

The astrocyte functions as a blood-brain barrier.

Nerve cell

Astrocytes determine which molecules are allowed to pass through the brain's cells. Chemotherapy drugs would normally not reach brain cells because of this blood-brain barrier. However, brain tumor patients receive a drug that temporarily inactivates the blood-brain barrier, allowing the drugs to pass through into the brain's cells.

This method allows for the administration of chemotherapy drugs directly into the cerebrospinal fluid. The Ommaya Reservoir is a small container that is surgically implanted under the scalp. A small tube extends from the reservoir into a ventricle, a hollow area of the brain that contains cerebrospinal fluid. Once the reservoir is in place, medications are injected into the reservoir with a syringe. The reservoir is then pumped to allow the flow of the medication throughout the central nervous system via the cerebrospinal fluid. The Ommaya Reservoir is significant not only because it avoids the blood-brain barrier, but also because it keeps chemotherapy drugs in the central nervous system and away from the rest of the body.

Side Effects of Treatment

Despite the availability of methods such as the Ommaya Reservoir, which are intended to minimize damage to healthy cells, all major treatments for brain tumors—surgery, radiotherapy, and chemotherapy—cause adverse side effects. Common side effects of treatment include extreme fatigue, edema (swelling in brain tissues), nausea and vomiting, diarrhea, and hair loss. While some of these effects are temporary or can be minimized by medications, their impact on patients who may still be dealing with lingering effects of their tumors can be overwhelming. In fact, many patients find the side effects of treatment much more uncomfortable than the original symptoms of their brain tumor. The mother of one brain tumor patient writes:

> There were times during my son's protocol that I felt he suffered more from the side effects of treatment than from the disease. It was emotionally painful for me to watch him go through so much. I think one of the hardest moments for me was the day he lost all his hair. Up until that point I had been living in a semi-state of denial. His bald head was more proof of our reality—he really did have cancer.[31]

Sometimes, medications given to counter side effects can have side effects of their own. For example, steroids, which effectively reduce edema, can cause problems such as stomach upset, mood swings, and increased susceptibility to infections. Steroids of the sort used to treat edema can also cause bones to weaken and can lead to loss of muscle tissue and weight.

The misery caused by side effects of treatment can be relentless. Furthermore, since chemotherapy is delivered through the bloodstream, side effects of chemotherapy tend to involve the patient's whole body. By contrast, the side effects of surgery and radiotherapy are mostly localized. Still, those side effects can be severe and debilitating.

Side Effects of Surgery

Some of the most extreme side effects accompany surgery. Tissues that were cut and abraded during surgery almost always swell. The swelling, what doctors call edema, may cause headaches, nausea, and blurred vision. Depending on the location of the tumor, patients may also have difficulties with speech, swallowing, memory, movement, and balance following surgery. These difficulties are sometimes temporary and disappear on their own. However, if the affected part of the brain was severely damaged, the patient may need long-term assistance or therapy aimed at relearning common skills such as walking or speech.

Even after their tumors are removed, some patients continue to experience seizures and some begin to experience them for the first time. These seizures are usually caused by scarring in brain tissues. A patient may need to take medications known as anticonvulsants indefinitely.

Side Effects of Radiotherapy

The swelling in brain tissues that follows surgery can also occur during radiotherapy. Patients exhibit the usual symptoms of edema, such as severe headaches, vomiting, and disturbance in vision. These adverse effects occur because just as radiation beams damage tumor cells, they also destroy healthy cells. Radiotherapy may cause skin and the mucous tissues in the nose and mouth to become inflamed. This inflammation results in decreased saliva production, mouth sores, and changes in the way taste buds work. Foods no longer taste the way they once did or seem to lose their flavor altogether. One patient complained, "The radiation . . . affected my sense of taste; everything I ate tasted like soap."[32]

Hair loss, another common effect of radiotherapy, typically occurs after three or four weeks of treatment. Dr. Myles Lampenfeld explains why hair loss occurs:

> At the base of . . . [the] hair shaft, in the hair follicle, there are rapidly dividing cells that make . . . hair grow. Radiation therapy damages those cells and causes hair loss in those areas exposed

Long-Term Side Effects of Radiotherapy in Children

Radiotherapy for children with brain tumors has been shown to cause side effects that are not observed for months or even years after treatment. For example, radiotherapy for pituitary gland tumors may cause side effects such as delayed growth, delayed or premature puberty, and difficulty or inability to have children. These effects occur because the pituitary gland, often called the "master gland," controls the secretion of hormones that regulate growth and development from childhood to adulthood.

Radiotherapy may also lower intellectual capacity—as measured by intelligence quotient (IQ) tests—in children. Moreover, studies have shown that IQs of very young children are more likely to suffer than IQs of older children treated with radiation. Radiotherapy for brain tumors may cause children to have additional difficulties in mental concentration, problems with speech, and learning disabilities. The severity of the problem often depends on the age of the patient. For example, a two-year-old child treated with radiation may have much more serious problems with speech than a seven-year-old child, because the two-year-old's treatment interrupts a crucial stage of speech development.

Radiotherapy also causes irradiated bones in the skull and face to stop growing. Since bones unaffected by radiation continue to grow, the heads and faces of irradiated children can appear uneven. Radiation to the head is also the only environmental risk linked conclusively to brain tumors. Therefore, doctors are especially cautious when prescribing radiotherapy for children, sometimes deciding to delay it or avoid it altogether.

to radiation. Hair loss can also occur on the opposite side of the body because of exit radiation. For instance, radiation treatment on one side of the head may cause hair loss on both sides because some of the radiation will go all the way through and affect the hair follicles on the opposite side.[33]

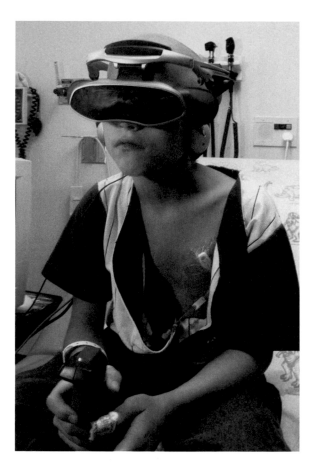

A young brain cancer patient plays a virtual reality game to distract himself while receiving chemotherapy, which causes painful side effects.

Side Effects of Chemotherapy

Like radiotherapy, chemotherapy damages normal cells as well as cancerous ones. Unlike radiotherapy, however, chemotherapy affects healthy cells throughout the body. These drugs, carried by the bloodstream, are particularly effective against rapidly dividing cells such as those found in tumors. The problem is that, during treatment, healthy cells that divide rapidly—including those in the digestive tract, hair follicles, and bone marrow (where blood cells are formed)—may be harmed. When these cells are damaged by chemotherapy, side effects such as nausea and vomiting, diarrhea or constipation, loss of hair, and anemia, due to damage to bone marrow, occur. Champion bicyclist Lance Armstrong, who received chemotherapy following surgical removal of two brain tumors, describes how "chemo" affected him:

Chemo doesn't just kill cancer—it kills healthy cells, too. It attacked my bone marrow, my muscle, my teeth, and the linings of my throat and my stomach and left me open to all kind of infections. My gums bled. I got sores in my mouth. And of course I lost my appetite, which was a potentially serious problem. Without enough protein, I wouldn't be able to rebuild tissue after chemo had eaten through my skin, my hair and my fingernails.[34]

Like side effects of other treatments, most of those caused by chemotherapy can be managed by medication. A more serious side effect, damage to bone marrow, may require that the patient receive a bone marrow transplant. Doctors sometimes prepare for the possibility of bone marrow destruction; they remove and save the patient's own marrow tissue prior to chemotherapy. They can then reintroduce the marrow when the patient needs it. If for some reason the patient's own marrow is unusable, bone marrow from a donor may be needed.

Whether caused by surgery, radiotherapy, or chemotherapy, side effects generally diminish as patients complete their prescribed treatment. Even as treatment ends, however, patients continue to face severe challenges as survivors of brain tumors. Besides coping with lingering effects of tumors themselves or their treatment, patients also must deal with the sense that a brain tumor is never completely cured. Peter, a patient with glioblastoma multiforme, writes:

I had always thought that if I lived after treatment was over I would be free of all this cancer stuff. I couldn't have been farther away from the truth. It seems that this cancer journey will not end until I am in my grave. I will always have this Brain Tumor thing over my head and I will never stop thinking about it or worrying that with every headache it is coming back. . . . I have to live every day of my life with this.[35]

CHAPTER FOUR

Follow-Up Care and Rehabilitation

In the case of many diseases, patients are said to be "cured" when the symptoms respond to treatment. In the case of brain tumors, however, the concept of being cured is not applicable. Instead, the brain tumor is said to be "in remission," meaning that it is not present at the time of examination. As Dr. Virginia Stark-Vance explains, "The word 'cure' is elusive because it is difficult to prove that a tumor will never recur, even after years of remission. There are some tumors that appear to be stable for months or years, only to later grow rapidly into a large mass."[36]

Since doctors cannot reliably predict whether or not a brain tumor will recur, lifelong monitoring is essential. In addition, to cope with cognitive and behavioral changes that result from the tumors themselves or their treatment, patients may need rehabilitation, educational and vocational counseling, psychological counseling, and assistance with day-to-day tasks that they previously could handle unaided.

Surviving Brain Tumors

Although doctors cannot predict with certainty the course of disease in an individual patient, they can provide patients with general information about expected outcomes based on factors such as the age of the patient, whether the tumor is primary or secondary, whether the tumor is benign or malignant, and the exact location of the tumor. For low-grade tumors such as benign meningiomas, for example, more than 85 percent of patients live at least five years after their initial diagnosis. For highly malignant tumors such as glioblastoma multiforme, this rate of survival is less than 5 percent.

Connor White (left), pictured here at a golf tournament in 2004, was successfully treated for brain cancer. The survival rate of children with brain tumors is higher than that of adults.

On the average, based on studies of patients with all types of brain tumors, approximately 30 percent of adult brain tumor patients and 70 percent of children with brain tumors survive at least five years after treatment. In determining the prognosis for an individual patient, however, the average survival rates do not necessarily apply. As Dr. Paul Zeltzer writes, "Prognoses are for groups of people. No doctor knows ahead of time who the survivors will be."[37]

While the prognosis of individual patients may be uncertain, what has become increasingly evident to health professionals is that patients need ongoing care after treatment ends. This is especially true for children, who may live for many years after successful treatment. These survivors may remain cancer-free but face medical and psychological challenges, some of which may not appear until years after treatment has ended. Dr. Fitzhugh Mullah, cofounder of the National Coalition for Cancer Survivorship, urges fellow doctors to continue caring for their patients after treatment, lamenting that "we have invented sophisticated techniques to save people from drowning, but once they have been pulled from the water, we leave them on the dock to cough and sputter on their own in the belief we have done all we can."[38]

Medical Follow-Up

Part of effective ongoing care for brain tumor patients is an examination by their doctors at least once every three months for the first year after treatment ends. Afterward, the frequency of

A brain tumor patient should be examined by his or her doctor every three months for the first year after treatment.

visits to the doctor can taper to two and then one per year. At these visits, patients undergo physical examinations, blood tests, imaging procedures such as MRI and CT scans, and other tests as necessary.

Follow-up care often includes controlling lingering effects of the tumors themselves or their treatment. Some patients, for example, need to continue taking antiseizure medications or steroids to control swelling of brain tissues. Children and adolescents who have undergone radiotherapy for pituitary gland tumors may need to take hormone treatments to prevent delays in puberty or premature puberty.

For some brain tumor survivors, especially those with benign tumors that were easily removed, life may eventually return to the way it was before diagnosis. For many patients, however, life after brain tumor treatment means dealing with a number of ongoing complications. One young woman describes the sweeping effects of her brain tumor and treatment:

> I'm 22 now and had an astrocytoma when I was 10. I had surgery, chemotherapy, and radiation to my head and spine. They ended up removing some of my vertebrae because I had so much tension from scoliosis and kyphosis [curvatures of the spine]. I get around in a wheelchair now. The radiation affected my ovaries and I'll never be able to have kids. I'm also pretty short (4'6") and skinny, but I try to eat nutritious food. I go to a healing center and exercise to try to keep a strong upper body. One of my legs is pretty bent, so the massage therapist works on that.[39]

For survivors such as this young woman, the need for support extends beyond medical follow-up. To help survivors who face complications, a number of rehabilitative services are available.

Rehabilitative Services

As side effects of treatment or as a direct result of their tumors, many brain tumor patients experience weakness, difficulty in movement, lack of coordination, and problems with swallowing and speech. The process of helping patients overcome these difficulties and adjust their daily routines is known as rehabilitation. The most common types of rehabilitative services for brain tumor patients are physical therapy, occupational therapy, and speech therapy.

Physical therapy consists of customized exercises to improve strength and motion in the arms or legs. Some patients use equipment such as stationary bicycles and treadmills to help them regain their strength. Other patients may be prescribed special swimming exercises.

Just as important as physical therapy is occupational therapy, which is aimed at helping patients relearn skills necessary for basic daily living. Occupational therapists help patients work on fine motor skills used in activities such as eating, dressing, combing hair, brushing teeth, and holding pens. Occupational therapists can also help patients who develop a condition known as sensory processing disorder. Patients with this disorder have difficulty with coordination and balance because they misinterpret certain sensory information such as touch, sound, and movement. Occupational therapists help these patients by teaching them to accurately interpret sensory information.

Speech therapy may be necessary for brain tumor patients whose speech and language skills have been affected, either by the tumor or its treatment. Some patients may have trouble understanding words, while others may be unable to vocalize words even though they know fully what they intend to say. Very young brain tumor patients may need speech therapy to help them overcome delays in speech development. Patients who develop difficulty swallowing following treatment are also referred to speech therapists because the muscles in the tongue and throat that are used in making sounds are the same muscles that are used in swallowing.

Educational and Vocational Assistance

In addition to physical disabilities, many patients find that their tumors or treatments have left them with cognitive impairments—that is, difficulties in understanding or processing new information. For students, cognitive impairments can show up as difficulty in paying attention, memorizing facts, reading, and comprehending what they read. These problems may be temporary or long-term. In either case, students with brain tumors need to be evaluated and given special educational help to make sure they do not fall behind in their academic progress.

Working adults may find that because of physical or cognitive disabilities they are unable to return to the same jobs they had before they fell ill. For example, patients who operated heavy machinery such as forklifts may not be able to resume their work because of the potential for accidents should they have seizures. Vocational counselors can help such patients discover new careers and learn new skills.

While some patients may need to change their jobs, experts say that it is important for them to remain involved in work or school if at all possible. According to psychologist Margaret Booth-Jones, "The ability to keep working or going to school may be as therapeutic as medication."[40]

Psychological Therapy

Another area in which brain tumor patients may need help is in managing their emotional response to their condition. Even after treatment ends, many patients continue to feel anxiety, anger, and sadness. In addition, survivors may suffer from a sense of loss, survival guilt, and fear of relapse.

Brain tumor survivors frequently feel that they cannot return to the life they had before their diagnosis. Although they are happy to be alive, they feel that survival has come at a great cost. One survivor, Michael, experienced loss of short-term memory and difficulty making good judgments. His wife describes Michael's emotional pain—as well as her own—in recognizing his loss:

> Michael . . . was very intelligent. The doctor told us these problems stemmed from a "host" of things such as the tumor itself, irradiation, and medication. Michael never fully regained his

remarkable intelligence, and this caused him so much pain, as he was quite aware he had deficits. . . . This disease can be really ugly and cruel. . . . I still find that I truly hate this . . . disease for what it robbed "us" of and most importantly, what it robbed him of.[41]

Many survivors also feel guilty about having lived through their disease and treatment when so many other patients do not. They might feel uncomfortable even discussing their problems when other patients have died. One patient says, "Survival guilt is a real problem. Often I find myself caught between needing to share my concerns and feeling guilty because I'm alive, I'm doing well, so many aren't. It's a tough line to walk."[42] Survivors might also feel guilty about the burden they feel they have placed on their families. One survivor explains:

My survivor's guilt has a different cause. I feel guilty about how much my need for high maintenance affects and limits my husband's choices about work, life and health insurance, where we live, how much extra money there is for recreation, how he has to go to many things by himself, how many chores I have to leave for him.[43]

Another common emotion among brain tumor survivors is fear that the tumor will recur. That fear, moreover, is often shared by the patient's loved ones. The mother of a child with a brain tumor describes how she felt when her child's treatment ended: "Finishing treatment was very difficult. I thought that I would feel like celebrating and cheering—but all I felt was fear. Treatment was over, but cancer was still a part of our lives. I think we will always live with the fear of relapse."[44]

Psychologists can help some patients deal with these emotions simply by listening. For some patients, just being able to express their feelings in a supportive environment is helpful in itself. Other patients find reassurance in learning that feelings of loss or guilt are normal responses to the situation they are in. Regardless of the patient's need, what is most helpful to patients is having someone with whom they can speak freely.

Psychological Impact of Brain Tumors on Families

When a member of a family or household has a brain tumor, all members—not just the patient—feel the impact. The brain tumor diagnosis creates a crisis in the family. As Dr. Jimmie Holland writes in the book *The Human Side of Cancer*, "Illness turns the status quo upside down." Roles and responsibilities in the family may shift whether or not people desire the change. In her lecture "Brain Tumors: Addressing Change at All Levels . . . It's a Family Thing," psychologist Margaret Booth-Jones provides examples: "The parent who was the disciplinarian or the parent who was the 'emotional glue' that held the family together" may have difficulty maintaining his or her role in the family after being diagnosed with a brain tumor.

Sometimes the spouse or parent of a patient needs to stop working in order to help the patient through the treatment. This frequently creates a financial crisis that is made worse by mounting medical bills. Financial burdens can add considerable emotional stress to families.

Children of patients may feel great fear and uncertainty about their parent's survival. Small children may even feel guilty about having caused their parent's illness, not realizing that they are not in any way responsible. Siblings of children with brain tumors may feel guilty about being well while their sibling is not. Healthy children may also worry that they, too, will develop brain tumors. While many healthy children are very protective toward their sick siblings, they may also be resentful and jealous of the extra attention that the sick child gets from their parents and other relatives.

Psychiatrist Jimmie Holland advises cancer patients, "Choose a therapist with whom you feel you can talk comfortably. The chemistry or rapport you feel with a particular therapist may be more important than the specific mode of therapy. The feeling of connectedness is key."[45]

Either with or without help, some patients manage to accept their new circumstances, even to the point of seeing a benefit from having had a brain tumor. One patient notes, "I've gained a lot of self-confidence from the cancer experience. Whenever there is a challenging obstacle to confront, I convince myself that if I survived the brain tumor, this is nothing! I've definitely become a much stronger person."[46]

While some patients manage to remain upbeat, others may find themselves overwhelmed despite psychotherapy. Patients

Brain tumor patients frequently suffer from depression and anxiety, which can be treated with counseling and medication.

may need medication to help them overcome anxiety or prolonged depression. Patients who experience severe impairment of mental processes or exhibit unusual behaviors may be referred to neuropsychologists. These specialists, using various assessment tests, can determine whether a patient's impairments and behaviors are caused by lingering effects of tumors and what rehabilitative measures are available.

Support Groups

While some patients benefit from one-on-one counseling, others find that support groups offer the emotional sustenance they need. These groups, which consist of patients, their families, and sometimes therapists, can offer help in person, by phone, or even via the Internet. According to Dr. Paul Zeltzer, connecting with support groups allows patients to "share the doubts, angst, and fears as well as celebrations of small successes that only people in the same situation would understand."[47] Dan, a brain tumor survivor, explains why attending support group meetings is important for him:

> For most people, you are basically doing this yourself and nobody around you has any idea what you are going through. But at these meetings, everyone is in the same boat, and they all know what you are going through. You don't have to feel funny if you are bald, or have trouble walking or talking. It's so easy to meet people and start up a conversation with "strangers," because you already have so much in common.[48]

Support from Family and Friends

In addition to aid from professionals and support groups, brain tumor patients often need assistance in their daily lives. It is crucial that they have the support of their family and friends in managing tasks such as taking medications, bathing, grooming, and dressing. Patients who suffer from seizures may need help with transportation since, in many states, people cannot legally drive unless they have been free of seizures for at least six months.

Help from a Friend

When Judy DiMaio's friend Elaine Vega was diagnosed with metastatic brain tumors, Judy moved into Elaine's home to help take care of her. In an interview with the author, Judy described how she helped Elaine and her family:

When I first moved in with Elaine, I didn't really think about what kind of help she needed. But I've thought about it since, and I would say that she needed help in four areas.

First, there was the need for physical care. I made sure she took her medications on time and let her doctors know if she had unusual reactions. I also gave her baths and helped her get dressed.

Second, Elaine needed social and intellectual stimulation. I would read to her or watch movies with her. We would do crossword puzzles and play games. She loved to e-mail friends, so I would help with that.

Third, I helped take care of the house, doing things that Elaine used to do before she got sick. I did laundry, got groceries, ran errands, made dinner—whatever needed to be done.

Fourth, I found that Elaine's husband and two boys needed support, too. I helped the boys with their homework and made sure they got ready for school in the morning. I took them to school and picked them up. The boys knew their mom was sick, and they knew that she might die, but I'm not sure they really understood it. So I spent time talking to them and also with their dad.

Brain tumor patients may also need assistance with tasks such as paying bills and handling correspondence. Many of them simply need the encouragement provided by caring family and friends. As brain tumor survivor David M. Bailey explains:

Treating a brain tumor is a complex thing—unlike a broken bone, you can't just treat the physical ailment—the tumor attacks who you are, and thus your intellect, feelings, and spirit are all threatened and must be cared for—and it's too much for one person to do it all, especially when you're fighting hard physically.[49]

Patients Helping Themselves

While the support of family, friends, and other patients is extremely valuable, brain tumor patients generally find that they must take responsibility for maintaining their own health. This means avoiding behaviors such as cigarette smoking and excessive sun exposure, which are known to cause cancer. Studies have shown that brain tumor survivors are at greater risk for second cancers and other diseases than is the general population. Survivors also need to avoid contact with people with infectious diseases, since the cancer therapies often weaken the

An instructor teaches yoga to cancer patients. Yoga can help give patients a feeling of calm and control.

immune system. Brain tumor survivors may need to take certain precautions to help them avoid seizures, such as getting adequate rest and eating regularly to prevent sudden drops in blood sugar levels. Patients may also be advised to avoid alcohol, nonprescription drugs, and activities that can cause overheating or sudden fluctuations in body temperature.

Paradoxically, exercise can be very beneficial to brain tumor patients by helping them regain their physical strength and stamina. Moreover, some forms of exercise, such as yoga and tai chi, can help patients achieve a sense of calm and control. Deep breathing, muscle relaxation, and meditation are additional practices that can make patients physically and psychologically more comfortable and at ease.

Exercises that are not overly vigorous are what survivors find most helpful. Following treatment, especially radiotherapy and chemotherapy, most patients feel weak and fatigued. Patients may also have lost a great deal of weight due to the nausea and vomiting that are common effects of tumors and their treatment and that make taking nourishment a chore. The point of exercise, then, is not to burn calories but to gain strength.

Palliative Care and Hospice

Despite the efforts of patients and health professionals, many brain tumor patients succumb to their disease. In some cases, doctors are not able to eliminate the tumors completely. In other cases, tumors are successfully removed, only to recur in the same place or elsewhere in the central nervous system. Doctors can try to treat the new tumors, but not every case will respond to additional surgery, radiotherapy, or chemotherapy. Moreover, some patients decide that the benefit from further treatment does not justify the additional discomfort they face.

In such cases, the doctors focus on providing the patient with palliative care. The word *palliative* refers to care that is intended to make the patient comfortable without attempting to cure the patient's disease. What this means in the care of a brain tumor patient is minimizing pain and controlling seizures, nausea and vomiting, and other symptoms.

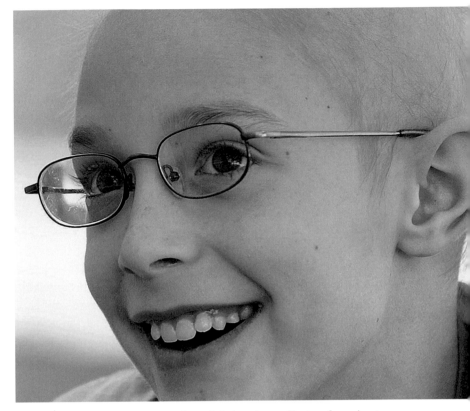

This young patient remains cheerful despite suffering from brain cancer. A positive outlook is crucial to a patient's chances of beating cancer.

Palliative care is usually provided through an institution known as hospice. In a hospice, specially trained staff do what they can to enhance the quality of the patient's remaining life. Hospice staff, including doctors, nurses, social workers, and other professionals, are also trained in helping patients and their families make the painful emotional adjustments to the patient's impending death. Such care may be offered either in a hospital-like facility or at home. The attendance of hospice staff at home allows the patient to die in familiar surroundings. If a patient's symptoms become so extreme that in-home care is no longer practical, hospices will transport the individual to a facility where more aggressive pain management is possible.

Beating the Odds

Given the overall poor rate of survival, the greatest challenge for brain tumor patients, their families, and their doctors is the maintenance of hope—believing that the odds can be beat. Yet hope is the most important ingredient in pursuing a cure. Dr. Nicholas de Tribolet recalls that his first brain tumor surgery was on a twenty-year-old man with glioblastoma multiforme. The prognosis for the patient was very poor, but Dr. de Tribolet convinced the patient and his family to pursue aggressive treatment. More than fifteen years later, the man was still alive, healthy, married, and the father of two children. Dr. de Tribolet notes:

> I learned from this experience that each patient should be given the chance to be an exception, whatever his or her prognosis may be. The neurosurgeon must not only provide the technical skill and clinical competence for treatment, but also the psychological prowess to convince the patient that there is a chance to survive, and that it is worthwhile to fight against the disease with all his or her energy. The patient and physician have to fight together.[50]

Just as Dr. de Tribolet and his patient fought together against a highly malignant brain tumor, so do many other doctors and patients. In order to help more patients beat the odds and win their fight, researchers are investigating several promising new therapies as well as improvements in the traditional therapies of surgery, radiotherapy, and chemotherapy.

CHAPTER FIVE

New Trends in Treatment

To achieve greater survival rates in brain tumor patients and to minimize side effects of treatment, scientists are designing innovations to the traditional therapies of surgery, radiotherapy, and chemotherapy. In addition, entirely new therapies are being investigated. The aim of these innovations and new therapies is to target tumor cells more precisely so as to avoid damage to healthy adjacent cells. Some of these therapies are already being used in medical centers that specialize in the treatment of brain tumors, while others are still being developed in laboratories.

One area scientists are working in is the refining of treatments already in use. Scientists are, for example, conducting clinical trials to investigate new ways of using drugs already known to be effective. Such trials involve using drugs in new combinations, changing the sequence of administering those drugs, or adjusting the dosage of the drugs. In other trials, researchers investigate whether tumors are best treated by a single therapy or a combination of therapies. For example, a study completed in 2004 compared the effectiveness of using radiation by itself to the effectiveness of using radiation along with a new drug known as Temodar. The study showed that 27 percent of patients who received Temodar along with radiation were still alive after two years, compared with only 10 percent of patients who survived after receiving radiation alone.

In 2004, these activists bicycled across the country in the Tour of Hope to urge public support for cancer research.

While the major goal of cancer researchers is to find ever more effective treatments of the cancer itself, according to science writer Robert Finn, "Not every cancer clinical trial is aimed squarely at finding a cure for the disease." Finn explains that "many clinical trials are intended to find treatments to alleviate some of the consequences of cancer or the side effects of some cancer treatments."[51] Current investigations in symptoms management include studies of pain relievers, antinausea medications, and treatments for dry-mouth syndrome, which commonly occurs in patients who receive radiation to the head.

All forms of traditional therapy for brain tumors—surgery, radiotherapy, and chemotherapy—are being enhanced by recent technological advances. Although these enhancements are not currently available in all hospitals, advances in technology have dramatically changed treatment in research hospitals and medical centers that specialize in the care of brain tumor patients.

Innovations in Surgery

Surgery to remove brain tumors has already made enormous strides since it began in the late nineteenth century. Then, over 50 percent of patients died during or immediately after surgery.

Clinical Trials

To improve survival odds for brain tumor patients, research is necessary to discover new medication and treatment techniques. In the United States, such research is sponsored by the National Cancer Institute and other governmental agencies. Drug companies and nonprofit organizations such as the American Brain Tumor Association and the National Brain Tumor Foundation also provide grants to researchers. Studies to investigate the effects of experimental drugs and treatments are known as clinical trials.

Participation in clinical trials is voluntary. Patients, however, must be willing to follow very precise instructions to help researchers make their evaluations. Before beginning a clinical trial, researchers study effects of the experimental therapy on laboratory animals. When results appear promising, studies begin on humans. Clinical trials are conducted in three steps known as phases. In Phase One, researchers test the treatment on a very small group of people to determine its safety. In Phase Two, testing the same treatment on a larger group of people, researchers try to determine its effectiveness. In Phase Three, testing the same treatment on an even larger group of people, researchers try to determine if the experimental therapy is better than existing treatments. If the experimental treatment is found to be safe, effective, and better than existing treatments, the therapy is then made available to other patients.

Today, despite the complexity of neurosurgery, less than 2 percent of patients die as a result of the surgery itself. Several factors, including the development of more precise surgical tools, the administration of antibiotics during surgery to prevent infection, and careful, continuous monitoring of patients have contributed to this vast improvement.

The factor that has most contributed to the safety of brain surgery in the last thirty years has been the availability of CT and MRI scans. Until the availability of these imaging technologies, neurosurgeons needed to perform "exploratory" surgeries during which they made large incisions and cut through multiple brain tissues in search of the tumor. With the advent of imaging scans, surgeons were able to aim precisely at the location of the tumor, thus avoiding unnecessary cuts. Innovations in MRI technology continue to offer neurosurgeons greater precision in reaching brain tumors.

One application of MRI technology that is becoming more widely used in large research hospitals is known as the intraoperative MRI. This innovation, which involves placing MRI equipment in the operating room, provides the neurosurgeon with a navigation guide during surgery. Although neurosurgeons routinely study MRI scans in planning surgeries, intraoperative MRI allows them to reach tumors with even greater precision. Operating room nurses Angela Kanan and Beth Gasson explain that imaging scans obtained prior to surgery "do not allow for the correction of brain shift," which occurs "when the dura [meninges] is opened, cerebrospinal fluid leaks out, and the brain either shrinks or swells."[52] The result is that the shape of the brain during surgery is slightly different from the shape shown in presurgery imaging scans. Being able to do a new MRI during surgery reduces the chance of errors that might result from relying on a presurgery scan and aids doctors in determining how much of the tumor has been removed.

Another form of MRI, known as functional magnetic resonance imaging (fMRI), is used prior to surgery either instead of or in addition to brain mapping. This imaging procedure measures the subtle changes that take place in the brain as a per-

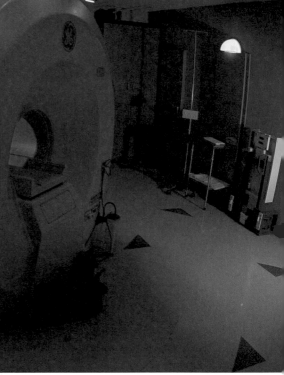

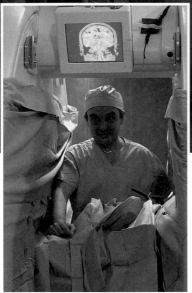

The use of intraoperative MRIs during brain tumor surgery allows doctors to operate with greater precision.

son performs certain tasks such as tapping fingers, speaking, or reading. When an area of the brain is hard at work, blood full of oxygen is rushed to the area. The fMRI scans show which part of the brain is receiving oxygenated blood as the task is being performed. This MRI technology assists the neurosurgeon in determining the location of eloquent functions of the cerebral cortex such as thought, speech, movement, and sensation.

Innovations in Radiotherapy

Just as neurosurgeons are using fMRI in mapping critical brain functions, radiation oncologists are using the same technology in planning stereotactic radiosurgeries. Functional MRIs help radiotherapists determine the best way to

Trends in Diagnosis

Innovations in MRI technology are providing neurosurgeons and radiation oncologists with greater precision in treating tumors. Similar innovations in MRI may also transform diagnostic procedures in the near future.

A variation of MRI known as magnetic resonance sprectroscopy (MRS) is being studied as an alternative to biopsies. Unlike regular MRIs that show tumors as undefined masses in the brain, MRS uses computers to analyze the chemical composition of masses. Knowing the chemical composition of the mass can help radiologists determine if the mass is a tumor. If MRS is proven to be as reliable and accurate as biopsy, the need for biopsy, which is an invasive surgical procedure, would be diminished.

Diffusion MRI is another form of MRI that can determine much earlier than conventional MRI or CT scans whether or not chemotherapy or radiotherapy is working. Through diffusion MRI, the movement of water molecules in brain tissues is traced before treatment and then traced again three weeks after the start of treatment. Tumor cells that have been destroyed by the treatment trap water molecules and change the results of the imaging scan. If tumor cells have not responded to the treatment, diffusion MRI shows no changes in the image. Doctors can thus determine that the therapy is not working and seek alternatives.

direct radiosurgical tools so that they avoid damage to eloquent areas of the brain.

Another innovation in radiotherapy intended to avoid radiation damage to healthy cells is a form of brachytherapy known as the Gliasite Radiation Therapy System. After a tumor is removed by surgery, an uninflated balloon, attached to a thin tube known as a catheter, is inserted in the cavity left by the removed tumor. Through the other end of the catheter, which extends out through the scalp, a liquid radioactive solution is allowed to drip into the balloon to fill it. As the balloon expands to touch the edges of the cavity, the radioactive solution begins to irradiate the immediate areas surrounding the cavity. This allows radiation to be concentrated on those areas most likely to contain cancer cells. Since the radiation affects only the immediate area of the tumor, the rest of the brain is spared the potentially damaging effects of radiation. The Gliasite system balloon usually stays in the patient for three to seven days, after which it is removed.

Innovations are also taking place in conventional radiotherapy. Researchers are experimenting with radiosensitizers, drugs that make tumor cells more sensitive to radiation. By combining radiosensitizers with radiation, doctors hope

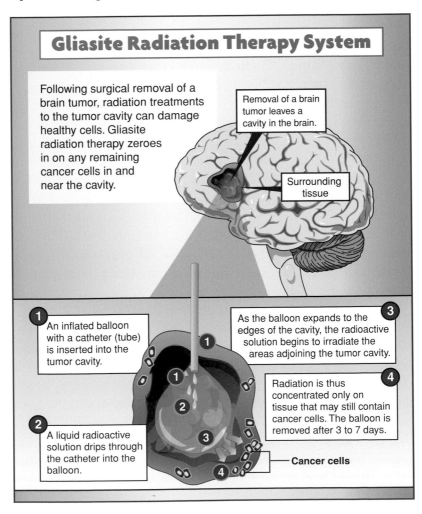

Gliasite Radiation Therapy System

Following surgical removal of a brain tumor, radiation treatments to the tumor cavity can damage healthy cells. Gliasite radiation therapy zeroes in on any remaining cancer cells in and near the cavity.

Removal of a brain tumor leaves a cavity in the brain.

Surrounding tissue

1 An inflated balloon with a catheter (tube) is inserted into the tumor cavity.

2 A liquid radioactive solution drips through the catheter into the balloon.

3 As the balloon expands to the edges of the cavity, the radioactive solution begins to irradiate the areas adjoining the tumor cavity.

4 Radiation is thus concentrated only on tissue that may still contain cancer cells. The balloon is removed after 3 to 7 days.

Cancer cells

to destroy tumor cells more effectively while using less radiation, thus minimizing side effects.

As an alternative to conventional radiotherapy, a few centers in the United States are offering proton therapy. Instead of using X-rays, this new therapy uses subatomic particles known as protons to destroy cancerous cells. The advantage of proton therapy over X-ray therapy is that it causes much less damage to healthy bones. Proton therapy may therefore be especially useful for treating children, whose skull and facial bones are still growing and could be vulnerable to damage from radiation.

Boron Neutron Capture Therapy

Another new form of radiotherapy, known as boron neutron capture therapy (BNCT), also seeks to destroy cancer cells without damaging healthy cells. Although this form of therapy has been widely tested in Japan it is now being tested in the United States only at Beth Israel Deaconess Medical Center in Boston, with assistance from the Massachusetts Institute of Technology (MIT). BNCT involves injecting the patient with a drug containing boron. The drug is especially designed to be absorbed by cancer cells only. Following injection with the drug, the patient is treated with radiation in the form of a neutron beam. When the neutron beams hit the boron atoms in the cancer cells, the atoms split, releasing subatomic particles that irradiate and destroy the cancer cells.

According to the BNCT researchers at MIT, because the radiation beams seek only those cells that have absorbed boron, "BNCT can be thought of as radiation therapy which targets cancer at the cellular level."[53] The advantage of radiation at the cellular level is that—unlike conventional radiotherapy, which damages both cancer and healthy cells—the healthy cells adjacent to the tumor avoid radiation and consequent damage. Researches think that BNCT may be especially useful in treating glioblastoma multiforme, which aggressively infiltrates healthy brain tissues and is extremely difficult to treat with conventional therapies.

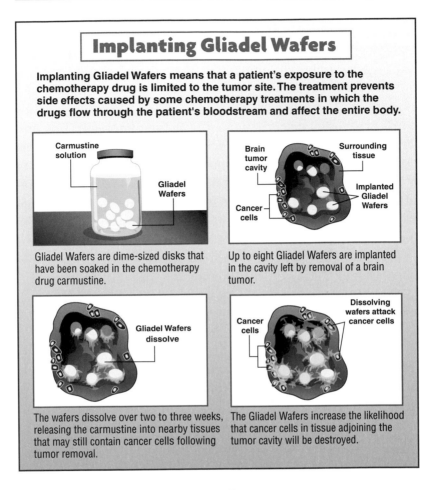

Implanting Gliadel Wafers

Implanting Gliadel Wafers means that a patient's exposure to the chemotherapy drug is limited to the tumor site. The treatment prevents side effects caused by some chemotherapy treatments in which the drugs flow through the patient's bloodstream and affect the entire body.

Carmustine solution

Gliadel Wafers

Gliadel Wafers are dime-sized disks that have been soaked in the chemotherapy drug carmustine.

Brain tumor cavity

Surrounding tissue

Cancer cells

Implanted Gliadel Wafers

Up to eight Gliadel Wafers are implanted in the cavity left by removal of a brain tumor.

Gliadel Wafers dissolve

The wafers dissolve over two to three weeks, releasing the carmustine into nearby tissues that may still contain cancer cells following tumor removal.

Cancer cells

Dissolving wafers attack cancer cells

The Gliadel Wafers increase the likelihood that cancer cells in tissue adjoining the tumor cavity will be destroyed.

Innovations in Chemotherapy

Avoiding damage to healthy cells is also one of the goals for researchers seeking to improve chemotherapy for brain tumors. A recent innovation is the Gliadel Wafer, a flat, dime-sized disk that is soaked in carmustine, a chemotherapy drug. Following surgical removal of a tumor, up to eight wafers are implanted in the tumor cavity. As the wafers dissolve over the subsequent two to three weeks, carmustine is released into the cells surrounding the wafers.

The Gliadel Wafer allows for a higher dose of the chemotherapy drug to be applied near the tumor area than would otherwise be possible. This may be especially advantageous in the treatment of highly malignant tumors. Since these tumors infiltrate nearby tissues, surgical removal of all tumor cells is usually not possible. By implanting the Gliadel Wafer, doctors increase the likelihood that remaining tumor cells are destroyed. At the same time, the Gliadel Wafer limits the patient's exposure to the chemotherapy drug to the tumor site. This limited exposure prevents side effects that occur when chemotherapy drugs course through the patient's bloodstream.

Another recently developed technique in the administration of chemotherapy is convection-enhanced delivery (CED). This technique is somewhat similar to the Gliasite system of delivering liquid radiation to the tumor site. In CED, thin catheters are placed near the tumor site during surgery. Over the next few days, chemotherapy drugs are delivered into the catheters and allowed to slowly drip into the tumor. Researchers are currently investigating the types of drugs that may be administered using CED as well as best methods for inserting the catheters.

Targeted Therapies

In addition to improved methods of delivering chemotherapy drugs to tumors, researchers are designing new classes of anticancer drugs. While traditional chemotherapy drugs aim to kill or prevent the replication of rapidly dividing cells—a category that includes tumor cells as well as normal ones—newer drugs are aimed at specific processes in tumor cells that allow them to thrive. For example, the drug Gleevec shuts off an enzyme known as tyrosine kinase that allows tumor cells to proliferate. Gleevec has been shown to be effective in treating a type of stomach cancer and a rare form of leukemia. Clinical trials are currently under way to determine if Gleevec is also effective in treating brain tumors.

While Gleevec is a chemotherapy drug, its action on a specific enzyme places it in a category of new anticancer agents known as targeted therapies. Since these therapies aim at specific processes in tumor cells, side effects like those that follow traditional chemotherapy are expected to be minimized. As biochemist Joseph Dooley and coauthor Marian Betancourt write, "The more that you can strike at cancer itself, the less harmful the cancer treatment can be."[54]

Angiogenesis Inhibitors

Another targeted therapy is angiogenesis inhibitors, which act against tumors by shutting off their supply of oxygen and nutrients. In 1971, Dr. Judah Folkman presented to the scientific community an idea he had worked on for about ten years. Dr. Folkman's idea was that tumors cause the formation of new blood vessels in a process he called angiogenesis. Folkman theorized that tumor cells released certain proteins, which he referred to as tumor angiogenesis factors, that caused adjacent

When mice with cancer are injected with endostatin, an angiogenesis inhibitor, their tumors nearly disappear.

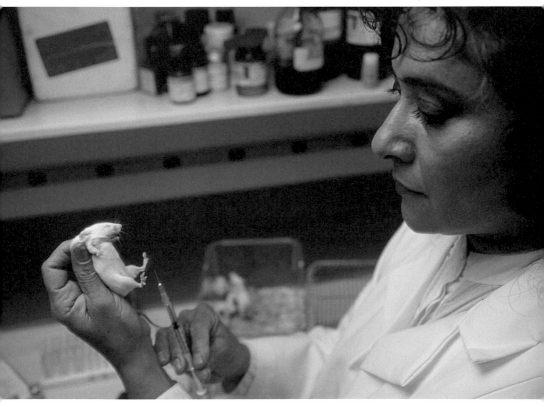

blood vessels to form new branches dedicated to supplying oxygen and nutrients to the tumor. Folkman suggested that shutting off the angiogenesis process would cause tumors to shrink.

Through years of research, Folkman and fellow investigators were able to identify more than a dozen angiogenesis factors. They also discovered that normal human cells have other factors, in addition to angiogenesis factors, that work to counter or inhibit angiogenesis. In laboratory tests on mice, researchers were able to demonstrate that when mice with tumors were injected with endostatin, one of the natural angiogenesis inhibitors, the tumors almost disappeared. Researchers are currently at work to determine if angiogenesis inhibitors can slow down or stop the growth of tumors in humans.

In testing angiogenesis inhibitors on humans, researchers are using both natural inhibitors and manufactured drugs. One drug, Avastin, which has proven to be effective in the treatment of colon cancer, is currently being studied in clinical trials to treat malignant gliomas. Another drug, Thalidomide, is now being studied as an angiogenesis inhibitor in brain tumors and other cancers. Thalidomide is controversial, however. Originally developed in the 1960s to counter nausea in pregnant women, it was banned when it was found to cause severe birth defects. In view of the drawbacks of Thalidomide as well as the promise of angioinhibitors, drug companies continue to search for other medications of this sort.

Gene Therapy

While researchers see hope in stopping the growth of tumors by cutting off their blood supply, other scientists hope to correct the faulty instructions that result in the growth of cancers in the first place. The objective is to use gene therapy to destroy the tumor cells at their most basic level.

In gene therapy, carriers known as vectors deliver new genetic instructions to tumor cells. Viruses have two characteristics that make them ideal vectors. First, viruses excel at invading human cells. Second, viruses are not able to reproduce unless they take over the replication process of the cells they invade. To take advantage of these characteristics of viruses, scientists modify them to make them harmless to normal cells, while loading them with instructions to destroy tumor cells. In effect, as journalist Alice Park writes, scientists turn viruses into "tiny Trojan horses that can sneak into tumor cells and destroy them from within."[55]

Scientists are currently studying a virus named ONYX-015, a common cold virus that has been altered so it can only invade human cells that lack the tumor suppressor gene p53. It is estimated that 50 percent of human tumors, including brain tumors, contain cells in which the p53 gene is either missing or damaged. In laboratory tests, ONYX-015 has invaded tumor cells, taken over their replication processes, and destroyed the cells. Researchers are currently testing the effect of ONYX-015 in human patients.

Scientists are also working to develop gene therapy to stop an enzyme in cancer cells known as telomerase. This enzyme is thought to interfere with regulators that determine how many times a cell divides and replicates. Normal human cells die after a set number of replications. That number ranges from fifty to sixty, depending on the type of cell. The presence of telomerase, however, ensures that cancer cells replicate indefinitely, thus becoming "immortal." While research on telomerase is at an early stage, according to Dooley and Betancourt, scientists hope to develop "ways to block telomerase in cancer cells to force them to age and die like normal cells."[56]

Immunotherapy

While traditional as well as newer therapies seek to act on tumor cells, immunotherapy seeks to stimulate the body's immune system to fight against tumors. Whenever the body is threatened by harmful invaders such as bacteria and viruses, the immune system, consisting primarily of white blood cells, springs into action. Although cancer cells are not invaders, scientists believe that the immune system can actually recognize tumor cells as harmful cells that need to be destroyed. According to doctors John Park and Christopher Benz,

For many years, physicians believed that the immune system was effective only in combating infectious diseases caused by such invading agents as bacteria and viruses. More recently, we have learned that the immune system may play a central role in protecting the body against cancer and in combating cancer that has already developed. This latter role is not well understood, but there is evidence that in many cancer patients the immune system slows down the growth and spread of tumors.[57]

Several forms of immunotherapy are being used or investigated in the treatment of cancer. The approach that is most widely used is treatment with cytokines. Cytokines are proteins produced by white blood cells when there is an infection or inflammation in the body. There are several naturally occurring cytokines, of which interferon has shown the greatest promise in the treatment of tumors.

There are very small amounts of interferon in the human body. Scientists, however, are able to synthesize three additional types of interferon. One form of interferon, interferon alpha, has been effective in treating cancers of the kidney, skin, muscles, and blood. Interferon alpha and a second form, interferon beta, are currently being investigated in clinical trials as treatments for brain tumors.

In addition to treatment with cytokines, researchers in immunotherapy are investigating several types of vaccines for cancer. Unlike vaccines for communicable diseases such as measles or polio, vaccines for cancer are not intended to prevent cancer but to assist the immune system in fighting cancer after it has occurred. To manufacture one form of cancer vaccine, tumor cells are removed from the patient being treated— or another patient with a similar tumor—and destroyed with radiation. The dead cells are then injected into the patients. Although the cells are dead, they contain antigens, substances that allow the immune system to recognize the cells as foreign invaders. The immune system recognizes the antigens and responds by attacking the dead cells as well as living cancer cells that contain the same antigens carried by the dead cells. Some

This young woman was able to graduate from high school despite suffering from brain cancer. Experts say that as new treatments are developed, the odds of surviving brain tumors will increase.

studies have shown cancer vaccines to be helpful, but much more research is needed before vaccination can be considered a consistently effective treatment of cancer.

Despite innovations in traditional treatments, and despite the hope that new therapies offer, brain tumors are likely to remain challenging diseases for years to come. As researchers discover more about the specific genes or cellular processes that trigger mutations, however, they hope to devise precise therapies that target those mutations and thus offer patients greater odds of surviving brain tumors.

Notes

Introduction: A Frightening Diagnosis

1. Jimmie C. Holland and Sheldon Lewis, *The Human Side of Cancer.* New York: HarperCollins, 2000, p. 133.
2. Terra Trevor, "Getting Through It: A Bridge to the Future," We Can Newsletter, Winter 2003. www.wecan.cc/newsletter2003winter.html.
3. Quoted in Paul Zeltzer, *Brain Tumors: Leaving the Garden of Eden.* Encino, CA: Shilysca, 2004, p. 23.
4. Tania Shiminski-Maher, Patsy Cullen, and Maria Sansalone, *Childhood Brain and Spinal Cord Tumors.* Sebastopol, CA: O'Reilly & Associates, 2002, pp. 6–7.
5. Roger S. Cicala, *The Brain Disorders Sourcebook.* Los Angeles: Lowell House, 1999, p. 145.

Chapter 1: Understanding Brain Tumors

6. Zeltzer, *Brain Tumors*, p. 311.
7. Sajeel A. Chowdhary, "Gliomas: Treatment Options and Rationale," Brain Tumor Talks Presentations, H. Lee Moffitt Cancer Center and Research Institute, December 9, 2004. www.moffitt.usf.edu/Prevention_and_Treatment/clinical_programs/neuro-oncology/index.asp#talks.
8. Chowdhary, "Gliomas."
9. Zeltzer, *Brain Tumors*, p. 233.
10. Virginia Stark-Vance, and Mary Louise Dubay, *100 Questions and Answers About Brain Tumors.* Sudbury, MA: Jones and Bartlett, 2004, p. 12.
11. Stark-Vance and Dubay, *100 Questions*, p. 10.
12. Cicala, *Brain Disorders*, p. 19.

Chapter 2: Diagnosis of Brain Tumors

13. David van Alstine, "How Tumors Cause Pain," in Roger S.

Cicala, *The Cancer Pain Sourcebook*. Lincolnwood, IL: Contemporary, 2001, p. 28.

14. Stark-Vance and Dubay, *100 Questions*, p. 21.
15. Shiminski-Maher, Cullen, and Sansalone, *Childhood Brain and Spinal Cord Tumors*, p. 281.
16. Cicala, *Brain Disorders*, p. 170.
17. Stanley Finger, *Minds Behind the Brain*. New York: Oxford University Press, 2004, p. 168.
18. Stanley Finger, *Origins of Neuroscience*. 2nd ed. New York: Oxford University Press, 2001, p. 438.
19. Cicala, *Brain Disorders*, p. 46.
20. Stark-Vance and Dubay, *100 Questions*, p. 52.
21. Cicala, *Brain Disorders*, p. 150.
22. Chowdhary, "Gliomas."

Chapter 3: Treatment of Brain Tumors

23. Chowdhary, "Gliomas."
24. Neil Feldstein, "Pediatric Neurosurgery," Columbia-Presbyterian Department of Neurological Surgery. http://cpmcnet.columbia.edu/dept/nsg/PNS/Tumors.html.
25. Zeltzer, *Brain Tumors*, p. 239.
26. Myles E. Lampenfeld, "What Is Radiation Therapy?" in Judith McKay and Nancee Hirano, *The Chemotherapy and Radiation Therapy Survival Guide*. Oakland, CA: New Harbinger, 1998, p. 19.
27. American Brain Tumor Association, *IMRT/Peacock System*, August 2001.
28. International RadioSurgery Association, "Stereotactic Radiosurgery Overview." www.irsa.org/radiosurgery.html.
29. International RadioSurgery Association, "Gamma Knife Surgery." www.irsa.org/gamma_knife.html.
30. Cicala, *Brain Disorders*, p. 209.
31. Quoted in Shiminski-Maher, Cullen, and Sansalone, *Childhood Brain and Spinal Cord Tumors*, p. 282.
32. Marie Beckerman, "Healing Is a Lifelong Process," in Tricia Ann Roloff, ed., *Navigating Through a Strange Land*. 2nd ed. Minneapolis: Fairview, 2001, p. 24.
33. Lampenfeld, "What Is Radiation Therapy?" p. 32.

34. Lance Armstrong with Sally Jenkins, *It's Not About the Bike: My Journey Back to Life*. 2nd ed. New York. Berkley, 2001, p. 129.

35. Peter D, "Brain Tumor Survivor: Peter D," Clinical Trials and Noteworthy Treatments for Brain Tumors. http://virtual trials.com/survivepeter.cfm.

Chapter 4:
Follow-Up Care and Rehabilitation

36. Stark-Vance and Dubay, *100 Questions*, p. 198.

37. Zeltzer, *Brain Tumors*, p. 43.

38. Quoted in Nancy Keene, Wendy Hobbie, and Kathy Ruccione, *Childhood Cancer Survivors*. Sebastopol, CA: O'Reilly & Associates, 2000, pp. 19–20.

39. Quoted in Keene, Hobbie, and Ruccione, *Childhood Cancer Survivors*, p. 239.

40. Margaret Booth-Jones, "Brain Tumors: Addressing Change at All Levels . . . It's a Family Thing." Brain Tumor Talks Presentations, H. Lee Moffitt Cancer Center and Research Institute, April 20, 2004. www.moffitt.usf. edu/Prevention_and_Treatment/clinical_programs/neuro-oncology/index.asp#talks.

41. Quoted in Zeltzer, *Brain Tumors*, p. 101.

42. Quoted in Keene, Hobbie, and Ruccione, *Childhood Cancer Survivors*, p. 43.

43. Quoted in Keene, Hobbie, and Ruccione, *Childhood Cancer Survivors*, p. 44.

44. Quoted in Shiminski-Maher, Cullen, and Sansalone, *Childhood Brain and Spinal Cord Tumors*, p. 431.

45. Holland and Lewis, *Human Side of Cancer*, p. 140.

46. Quoted in Keene, Hobbie, and Ruccione, *Childhood Cancer Survivors*, p. 55.

47. Zeltzer, *Brain Tumors*, p. 28.

48. Quoted in Zeltzer, *Brain Tumors*, p. 61.

49. David M. Bailey, "Brain Tumor Survivor: David M. Bailey," Clinical Trials and Noteworthy Treatments for Brain Tumors. http://virtualtrials.com/survivedavid.cfm.

50. Nicholas de Tribolet, "The Patient and Physician Must Fight Together," in Roloff, *Navigating Through a Strange Land*, p. 129.

Chapter 5: New Trends in Treatment

51. Robert Finn, *Cancer Clinical Trials*. Sebastopol, CA: O'Reilly & Associates, 1999, p. 84.

52. Angela Kanan and Beth Gasson, "Brain Tumor Resections Guided by Magnetic Resonance Imaging," *AORN Journal*, March 2003, p. 583. www.findarticles.com/p/articles/mi_m 0FSL/is_3_77/ai_99237600.

53. MIT Nuclear Reactor Laboratory, "Boron Neutron Capture Therapy Research," http://mit.edu/nrl/www/bnct/re search/.

54. Joseph F. Dooley and Marian Betancourt, *The Coming Cancer Breakthroughs*. New York: Kensington, 2002, p. 17.

55. Alice Park, "When Bad Bugs Go Good," *Time*, March 28, 2005.

56. Dooley and Betancourt, *Coming Cancer Breakthroughs*, p. 37.

57. John W. Park and Christopher C. Benz, "Immunotherapy Cancer Treatment," Cancer Supportive Care Programs, 2001. www.cancersupportivecare.com/immunotherapy. html.

Glossary

anesthesia: The administration of medications to make patients unconscious or pain-free during surgical procedures.

angiogenesis: The formation of new blood vessels.

anticonvulsant: Medication used to treat or prevent seizures.

astrocyte: A star-shaped glial cell that supports neurons in the central nervous system.

axons: Thin, long fibers of neurons that send out signals.

benign brain tumor: A brain tumor that grows slowly and does not infiltrate nearby tissues.

biopsy: Surgical removal of a small amount of tissue to be examined by a pathologist.

blood-brain barrier: The protective barrier between the blood vessels and the tissues of the brain. Chemotherapy drugs must cross the barrier in order to reach tumors.

brachytherapy: A method of internal radiation treatment in which radioactive substances are placed near a brain tumor during surgery.

brain stem: The part of the brain that connects the brain to the spinal cord. It is responsible for involuntary vital functions such as breathing and heartbeat.

cerebellum: Part of the brain that is responsible for balance and coordination of movement. It is located in the back of the head, under the cerebrum.

cerebrospinal fluid: The protective liquid that surrounds both the brain and the spinal cord.

cerebrum: The top and largest portion of the brain. It is divided into two hemispheres. It controls thought, sensory perception, language processing, speech, and voluntary movement.

chemotherapy: A type of treatment in which drugs are used to destroy tumor cells.

clinical trial: A study designed to determine the safety and effectiveness of a new treatment.

computed axial tomography (CAT or CT): An imaging technique used in the diagnosis of brain tumors in which an X-ray device linked to a computer produces images of cross-sections of the brain.

craniotomy: Surgery of the cranium, or skull.

debulking: Partial surgical removal of a tumor.

ependymal cell: A type of glial cell that lines the ventricles of the brain and the central canal of the spinal cord.

gene: Inherited factor that determines traits in an organism. Tumors begin when faulty instructions from genes cause cells to mutate.

gene therapy: Treatment that seeks to repair or replace defective genes.

glial cells: Cells of the central nervous system that nourish and support the neurons, or nerve cells. Astrocytes, oligodendrocytes, and ependymal cells are types of glial cells.

glioma: A general term that describes any tumor that contains glial cells.

grade: A designation to identify the aggressiveness of a tumor. Grades are usually expressed in Roman numerals ranging from I (least aggressive) to IV (most aggressive).

immune system: The body's defense system that protects it from harmful foreign substances such as bacteria and viruses.

immunotherapy: A treatment that stimulates the body's immune system to fight infection and disease.

lumbar puncture: A diagnostic procedure in which a sample of cerebrospinal fluid is withdrawn from the spine. Also known as a spinal tap.

magnetic resonance imaging (MRI): An imaging technique used in the diagnosis of brain tumors in which magnets and radio waves are used to produce computerized images of the brain.

malignant brain tumor: A brain tumor that has cancerous cells, grows rapidly, or aggressively infiltrates nearby tissues.

meninges: Three layers of protective membranes that cover the brain and spinal cord.

metastatic brain tumor: A cancer that originates elsewhere in the body and then travels to the brain. Also known as a secondary brain tumor.

mutation: A change in cells caused by faulty instruction from genes.

neurons: Nerve cells of the central nervous system that receive and transmit impulses.

oligodendrocyte: A type of glial cell that insulates neurons by forming a sheath around axons.

oncogenes: Genes that can transform a cell into a tumor cell.

positron emission tomography (PET): An imaging technique used in the diagnosis of brain tumors in which the activity of tumors is tracked.

primary brain tumor: A type of tumor that originates from the cells of the brain itself, as opposed to metastatic or secondary tumors that originate elsewhere in the body and then travel to the brain.

protocol: A plan that specifies exact medications, dosages, and procedures to be followed in a particular treatment.

proton therapy: A form of radiotherapy that uses proton beams instead of X-rays.

radiotherapy: The use of radiation beams on tumors in order to stall their growth.

remission: The disappearance of a tumor.

resection: Surgical removal of a tumor.

Schwann cells: Cells that insulate and protect the peripheral nerves.

seizure: An involuntary jerking of muscles that may involve part or all of the body. Also known as a convulsion.

tumor: An abnormal mass of tissue that may be benign or malignant.

ventricles: Fluid-filled cavities of the brain in which cerebrospinal fluid is manufactured.

Organizations to Contact

American Brain Tumor Association

2720 River Rd., Des Plaines, IL 60018
(800) 886-2282
e-mail: info@abta.org
www.abta.org

The American Brain Tumor Association provides information and support to brain tumor patients and their families. This organization distributes many booklets on brain tumors and their treatment. The Web site includes a page where young people with brain tumors can share their stories or read the stories of other young brain tumor patients.

American Cancer Society

1599 Clifton Rd. NE, Atlanta, GA 30329
(800) 227-2345
www.cancer.org

The American Cancer Society is one of the oldest and largest health support organizations. Through its publications and Web site, it provides statistics and information about all types of cancers and their treatment.

Candlelighters Childhood Cancer Foundation

PO Box 498, Kensington, MD 20895-0498
(800) 366-2223
e-mail: staff@candlelighters.org
www.candlelighters.org

The Candlelighters Childhood Cancer Foundation was founded by parents of children with cancer. This organization provides support and education for children and adolescents with cancer and their families.

Musella Foundation for Brain Tumor Research and Information

1100 Peninsula Blvd., Hewlett, NY 11557
(516) 295-4740
(888) 295-4740
e-mail: musella@virtualtrials.com
www.virtualtrials.com

Through its Web site, this foundation provides information on brain tumors and available treatments and clinical trials. Also available on the Web site are stories from survivors of brain tumors, links to support groups, and informative newsletters.

National Brain Tumor Foundation

22 Battery St., Suite 612, San Francisco, CA 94111-5520
(415) 834-9970
e-mail: nbtf@braintumor.org
www.braintumor.org

This organization offers information regarding brain tumors and their treatment. It also maintains a database of medical centers that specialize in the care and treatment of brain tumors.

National Children's Cancer Society

1015 Locust, Suite 600, St. Louis, MO 63101
(314) 241-1600
e-mail: krudd@children-cancer.org
www.nationalchildrenscancersociety.com

The National Children's Cancer Society provides educational information and support to children with cancer and their families. This organization also offers financial assistance to qualified families to meet medical and nonmedical costs of caring for children with cancer.

National Coalition for Cancer Survivorship (NCCS)

1010 Wayne Ave., Suite 770, Silver Spring, MD 20910
(301) 650-9127
e-mail: info@canceradvocacy.org
www.cansearch.org

The NCCS is an organization dedicated to supporting long-term survivors of cancer and to making their needs known to the greater public.

National Institutes of Health (NIH)

9000 Rockville Pike, Bethesda, MD 20892
(301) 496-4000
e-mail: nihinfo@od.nih.gov
www.nih.gov

The NIH is the primary U.S. government agency for conducting and supporting health research. Two of its twenty-seven institutes and centers are the National Cancer Institute (www.cancer.gov) and the National Institute of Neurological Disorders and Stroke (www.ninds.nih.gov). Both these institutes provide information regarding brain tumors in books, in pamphlets, and online. The NIH also maintains a Web site regarding all ongoing clinical trials (www.cancer.gov/clinicaltrials).

We Can, Pediatric Brain Tumor Network

PO Box 614, Manhattan Beach, CA 90266
(310) 739-3433
e-mail: emailgigi@wecan.cc
www.wecan.cc

We Can is an association that provides support to families of children with brain tumors. The association sponsors social gatherings, special workshops for teens and siblings of patients, and group meetings where members share information and provide each other with emotional support. Members can also receive support by phone or by e-mail.

For Further Reading

Books

Elena V. Dorfman, *The C-Word: Teenagers and Their Families Living with Cancer.* 2nd ed. Troutdale, OR: NewSage, 1998. This book includes stories and photographs of five teenagers who survived cancer.

Kathleen Gay and Sean McGarrahan, *Epilepsy: The Ultimate Teen Guide.* Lanham, MD: Scarecrow, 2002. The term *epilepsy* is used to describe recurrent seizures. Seizures may be caused by several diseases including brain tumors. This book describes how seizures occur, how they are diagnosed and treated, and how people, including coauthor McGarrahan, live and cope with seizures.

Karen Gravelle and Charles Haskins, *Teenagers Face to Face with Cancer.* Lincoln, NE: iUniverse, 2000. Sixteen teenagers describe the impact of cancer on their lives, their relationships with family and friends, and their plans for the future.

Chris Hayhurst, *The Brain and Spinal Cord: Learning How We Think, Feel, and Move.* New York: Rosen, 2002. The author describes the brain and nervous system and provides detailed illustrations based on computer scans of human bodies.

Carla Killough McClafferty, *The Head Bone's Connected to the Neck Bone: The Weird, Wacky, and Wonderful X-ray.* New York: Farrar, Straus, and Giroux, 2001. The author describes William Roentgen's discovery of the X-ray, its history, and its uses today.

Julie McDowell, *The Nervous System and Sense Organs.* Westport, CT: Greenwood, 2004. The author discusses the central and peripheral nervous systems and the interactions of the nervous system with the sense organs. The book also contains a history of scientific discoveries related to the nervous system and a chapter on Nobel Prize winners whose works advanced neuroscience.

Lisa Yount, *Cancer.* San Diego: Lucent, 1999. This book describes the nature of cancer, its probable causes, its diagnosis, and its treatment.

Web Sites

How Stuff Works (www.howstuffworks.com). This Web site provides descriptions of various technologies, including MRI, CT, and PET scans.

Neuroscience for Kids (http://faculty.washington.edu/chudler/neurok.html). This Web site provides comprehensive information about the nervous system, including the brain, the spinal cord, neurons and glial cells, disorders of the nervous system, and methods of study in neuroscience.

RadiologyInfo (www.radiologyinfo.org). This site provides information on X-rays, CTs, MRIs, and radiation therapy. Available on the Web site are short, animated videos showing various imaging techniques as well as pictures of scans and scanning machines.

Works Consulted

Books

American Brain Tumor Association, *A Primer of Brain Tumors*. 8th ed. ABTA, 2004. This booklet provides an overview of brain tumors, their symptoms, and their treatment.

Lance Armstrong with Sally Jenkins, *It's Not About the Bike: My Journey Back to Life*. 2nd ed. New York: Berkley, 2001. The authors describe Armstrong's diagnosis, treatment, and recovery from cancer, including metastatic brain cancer.

Jackson Beatty, *The Human Brain: Essentials of Behavioral Neuroscience*. Thousand Oaks, CA: Sage, 2001. The author describes in detail the anatomy and function of the human brain.

Central Brain Tumor Registry of the United States, *Statistical Report: Primary Brain Tumors in the United States, 1997–2001*. CBTRUS, 2004. This booklet contains statistical reports regarding the prevalence of brain tumors in various demographic groups.

Roger S. Cicala, *The Brain Disorders Sourcebook*. Los Angeles: Lowell House, 1999. The author discusses several disorders that can impact the brain, including brain tumors.

——, *The Cancer Pain Sourcebook*. Lincolnwood, IL: Contemporary, 2001. The author, along with several contributors, discusses how cancer pain occurs and how medications can minimize it.

Joseph F. Dooley and Marian Betancourt, *The Coming Cancer Breakthroughs*. New York: Kensington, 2002. The authors discuss several treatments for cancer currently under investigation, including gene therapy, immunotherapy, and angiogenesis inhibitors.

Stanley Finger, *Minds Behind the Brain*. New York: Oxford University Press, 2004. The author relates the history of neuroscience through biographical discussions of the scientists who made significant discoveries about the brain.

———, *Origins of Neuroscience.* 2nd ed. New York: Oxford University Press, 2001. The author provides a comprehensive history of neuroscience from ancient cultures to the present.

Robert Finn, *Cancer Clinical Trials.* Sebastopol, CA: O'Reilly & Associates, 1999. This book describes clinical trials and provides patients with information on how to select and join them.

Jimmie C. Holland and Sheldon Lewis, *The Human Side of Cancer.* New York: HarperCollins, 2000. Dr. Holland, a psychiatrist who specializes in the care of cancer patients, and her coauthor discuss the psychological and social issues that face cancer patients and their families.

Nancy Keene, Wendy Hobbie, and Kathy Ruccione, *Childhood Cancer Survivors.* Sebastopol, CA: O'Reilly & Associates, 2000. The authors discuss the issues that face children who survive cancers, including brain tumors.

Judith McKay and Nancee Hirano, *The Chemotherapy and Radiation Therapy Survival Guide.* Oakland, CA: New Harbinger, 1998. The authors describe common side effects of chemotherapy and radiotherapy and recommend coping strategies.

National Brain Tumor Foundation, *The Essential Guide to Brain Tumors.* NBTF, 2004. This booklet describes the human brain, the diagnosis of brain tumors, their treatment, and issues facing survivors.

Tricia Ann Roloff, ed., *Navigating Through a Strange Land.* 2nd ed. Minneapolis: Fairview, 2001. Editor Roloff presents in this book a collection of essays written by patients, family members, and health care professionals regarding brain tumors.

Tania Shiminski-Maher, Patsy Cullen, and Maria Sansalone, *Childhood Brain and Spinal Cord Tumors.* Sebastopol, CA: O'Reilly & Associates, 2002. This comprehensive book covers central nervous system tumors that affect children. The authors provide concrete information about brain tumors, their symptoms, their treatment, hospital procedures, and various issues that face patients and their families.

Virginia Stark-Vance and Mary Louise Dubay, *100 Questions and Answers About Brain Tumors*. Sudbury, MA: Jones and Bartlett, 2004. This book, written in a question-and-answer format by a neuro-oncologist and a brain tumor patient, provides comprehensive information regarding the diagnosis and treatment of brain tumors.

Paul Zeltzer, *Brain Tumors: Leaving the Garden of Eden*. Encino, CA: Shilysca, 2004. This book is addressed to brain tumor patients and gives them information about various brain tumors as well as tips on finding qualified health care providers.

Fact Sheets and Pamphlets

American Brain Tumor Association, *Boron Neutron Capture Therapy*, November 2003.

———, *Chemotherapy*, 2004.

———, *Conventional Radiation Therapy*, 2004.

———, *IMRT/Peacock System*, August 2001.

———, *Stereotactic Radiosurgery*, 2002.

———, *Surgery*, 2004.

Proxima Therapeutics, "Gliasite Radiation Therapy System," 2001.

Periodicals

Jean Marx, "Encouraging Results for Second-Generation Antiangiogenesis Drugs," *Science*, May 27, 2005.

Thomas H. Maugh II, "New Pains for Adult Survivors of Childhood Cancer," *Los Angeles Times*, May 18, 2005.

Alice Park, "When Bad Bugs Go Good," *Time*, March 28, 2005.

Internet Sources

David M. Bailey, "Brain Tumor Survivor: David M. Bailey," Clinical Trials and Noteworthy Treatments for Brain Tumors. http://virtualtrials.com/survivedavid.cfm.

Margaret Booth-Jones, "Brain Tumors: Addressing Change at All Levels . . . It's a Family Thing," Brain Tumor Talks Presentations, H. Lee Moffitt Cancer Center and Research Institute, April 20, 2004. www.moffitt.usf.edu/Prevention_and_Treatment/clinical_programs/neurooncology/index.asp#talks.

Sajeel A. Chowdhary, "Gliomas: Treatment Options and Rationale," Brain Tumor Talks Presentations, H. Lee Moffitt Cancer Center and Research Institute, December 9, 2004. www.moffitt.usf.edu/Prevention_and_Treatment/clinical_programs/neuro-oncology/index.asp#talks.

Nicole Fawcett, "New Imaging Method Gives Early Indication If Brain Cancer Therapy Is Effective, U-M Study Shows," University of Michigan Health System, March 29, 2005. www.med.umich.edu/opm/newspage/2005/braincancer.htm.

Neil Feldstein, "Pediatric Neurosurgery," Columbia-Presbyterian Department of Neurological Surgery. http://cpmcnet.columbia.edu/dept/nsg/PNS/Tumors.html.

International RadioSurgery Association, "Gamma Knife Surgery." www.irsa.org/gamma_knife.html.

———, "Stereotactic Radiosurgery Overview." www. irsa.org/radiosurgery.html.

Angela Kanan and Beth Gasson, "Brain Tumor Resections Guided by Magnetic Resonance Imaging," *AORN Journal*, March 2003. www.findarticles.com/p/articles/mi-m0FSL/is_3_77/ai_99237600.

Kevin C. Oeffinger and Melissa M. Hudson, "Long-term Complications Following Childhood and Adolescent Cancer: Foundations for Providing Risk-based Health Care for Survivors," *CA: A Cancer Journal for Clinicians*, July/August 2004. http://caonline.amcancersoc.org/cgi/content/full/54/4/208.

John W. Park and Christopher C. Benz, "Immunotherapy Cancer Treatment," Cancer Supportive Care Programs, 2001. www.cancersupportivecare.com/immunotherapy.html.

Ransdell Pierson, "Schering-Plough Brain Cancer Drug Wins Expanded OK," Clinical Trials and Noteworthy Treatments for Brain Tumors, March 16, 2005. http://virtualtrials.com/news3.cfm?item=3052.

Aileen Staller, "Seizures: What You Want to Know But Were Afraid to Ask," Brain Tumor Talks Presentations, H. Lee Moffitt Cancer Center and Research Institute, March 23, 2004. www.moffitt.usf.edu/Prevention_and_Treatment/clinical_pro grams/neuro-oncology/index.asp#talks.

Terra Trevor, "Getting Through It: A Bridge to the Future," We Can Newsletter, Winter 2003. www.wecan.cc/newsletter2003 winter.html.

Web Sites

American Brain Tumor Association (www.abta.org). This Web site contains extensive information about brain tumors, their diagnosis, and their treatment. Several of the organization's publications are available online.

Angiogenesis Foundation (www.angio.org). This Web site contains information about the theory of angiogenesis and ongoing research on angiogenesis inhibitors.

Clinical Trials and Noteworthy Treatments for Brain Tumors (www.virtualtrials.com). This Web site provides information on brain tumors, clinical trials, stories of brain tumor survivors, and chat rooms, including a chat room for teens and young adults.

International Radiosurgery Association (www.irsa.org). This Web site provides an overview of brain tumors and radiotherapy, along with specific information about radiosurgery and radiosurgical tools and procedures.

H. Lee Moffitt Cancer Center and Research Institute (www.moffitt.usf.edu). This Web site contains information and resources about various cancers, including brain tumors. Several lectures by health care professionals who treat brain tumor patients are available at www.moffitt. usf.edu/Prevention_and_Treatment/clinical_programs/neuro-oncology/index.asp#talks.

Index

aggressiveness, 15–17
allergens, 25
Alstine, David van, 32–33
American Brain Tumor
  Association, 27–28, 50, 77
angiogenesis, 23, 86
angiogenesis inhibitors,
  85–86
angiogram, 41
anticonvulsants, 56
antigens, 88–89
Armstrong, Lance, 9–10, 58–59
astrocytes, 18
Avastin, 86
axons, 18

benign tumors, 15, 16–17
Benz, Christopher, 87–88
Betancourt, Marian, 84–85, 87
biopsy, 42, 43–44
blood-brain barrier, 53–55
bone marrow transplant, 59
Booth-Jones, Margaret, 65, 67
Boron Neutron Capture
  Therapy (BNCT), 82
brachytherapy, 52
brain, 26, 27, 47
  complexity of, 10–11
"Brain Tumors: Addressing
  Change at All Levels"
  (Booth-Jones), 67
brain tumors, 39, 59, 67
  age factor and, 28–29
  classifications of, 15–22
  emotional responses to,
    10–12

history of medicine
  involving, 36–38
  terms for, 14–15
Broca, Paul, 37, 38

cancer cell enzymes, 87
carmustine, 83
CAT. *See* computed axial
  tomography
causes, 24–25
cells
  in brain tumor formation
    process, 22–23
  types of, 18–19
Central Brain Tumor Registry
  of the United States, 18
central nervous system, 14,
  18–19, 20–21
cerebrospinal fluid, 18,
  20–21, 43–44
  blockage of, 30–31
  examination of, for
    diagnosis, 43–44
  functions of, 18, 20–21
chemotherapy, 52–53, 58–59,
  83–86
Chowdhary, Sajeel, 17, 45, 44
Cicala, Roger, 13, 29, 35, 38,
  44, 53
cigarette smoking, 25–26
clinical trials, 77
closed biopsy, 43
computed axial tomography
  (CAT or CT), 40
convection-advanced
  delivery (CED), 84

craniotomy, 46–47
cure, 60, 88–89
cytokines, 88
cytostatic drugs, 53
cytotoxic drugs, 53

debulking, 46
diagnosis
   history of, 36–37
   symptoms and, 30, 30–36
   tests used in, 40–44
diet, 24
doctors, 39
Dooley, Joseph, 84–85, 87
drugs. *See* medications

educational assistance, 64–65
emotional responses, 65–69
environmental factors, 24
enzymes, 87
ependymal cells, 18

Feldstein, Neil, 46
Finger, Stanley, 37–38
Finn, Robert, 76
Folkman, Judah, 85–86
follow-up, 62–63
formation, process, 22–23
functional magnetic
   resonance imaging (fMRI),
   78–79

Gamma Knife, 51–52
Gasson, Beth, 78
gene therapy, 86–87
Gleevec, 84
Gliadel Wafer, 83–84
glial cells, 18
Gliasite Radiation Therapy
   System, 80–81
growth process, 23

headaches, 31–33

heredity, 25
history, of medicine, 36–38
Holland, Jimmie, 11, 67
hope, 74
hospice, 72, 73
Human Side of Cancer, The
   (Holland), 67

imaging tests, 40–44
immune system, 87–89
immunotherapy, 87–89
intensity modulated radiation
   therapy (IMRT), 50
interferon, 88
internal radiotherapy, 52
International RadioSurgery
   Association (IRSA), 51–52
intracranial pressure, 30–31,
   49
intracranial tumors, 14

Kanan, Angela, 78

Lampenfeld, Myles, 50,
   56–57
Lister, Joseph, 37, 38
lumbar puncture, 43–44

Macewan, William, 38
magnetic resonance imaging
   (MRI), 40, 78
malignant tumors, 15, 16
medications
   angiogenesis inhibitors,
      85–86
   chemotherapy, 83–86
   for immunization against
      cancer, 87–89
   for use with radiation
      treatment, 75, 81–82
   see also clinical trials
meninges, 19, 33
metastatic brain tumors, 17, 28

morbidity, 46
MRI. *See* magnetic resonance imaging
Mullahy, Fitzhugh, 62
mutation, 22–23
myelon, 18

National Brain Tumor Foundation, 77
National Coalition for Cancer Survivors, 62
nausea, 31, 33
neurologists, 39
neurons, 18
neuro-oncologists, 39
neuropathologists, 39
neuroradiologists, 39
neurosurgeons, 39, 78–79
nitrates, 24

occupational therapy, 64
oligodendrocytes, 18
Ommaya Reservoir, 53–55
oncogenes, 22–23
ongoing care, 74
   family and friends' support and, 69–71
   medical follow-up in, 62–63
   necessity for, 60–62
   psychological therapy during, 65–69
   rehabilitative services in, 63–65
   self-help and, 71–72
ONYX-015, 87
open biopsy, 43

pain sensors, 47
palliative care, 72–73
Park, Alice, 87
Park, John, 87–88
peripheral nervous system, 20–21

physical therapy, 64
physicians, 39
pineal glands, 19
pituitary glands, 19
pituitary tumors, 49
positron emission tomography (PET), 40–41
primary brain tumors, 17
primary malignant brain tumors, 28
proton therapy, 82
psychological therapy, 65–66

radiation. *See* radiotherapy
radiation oncologist, 39
radiosensitizers, 81–82
radiosurgery, 50-52
radiotherapy, 24, 49, 50
   side effects from, 56–57
   technological advances in, 79–83
rehabilitative services, 63–65
remission, 60
research, 75, 77
   see also technological advances
resection, 45
Roentgen, William, 38

Schwann cells, 19
secondary brain tumor, 17
seizures, 33–34, 56
self-help, by survivors, 71–72, 74
Seltzer, Paul, 46
shunt implantation, 49
side effects
   chemotherapy related, 58–59
   general characteristics of, 55–56
   radiotherapy related, 56–57

smoking. *See* cigarette smoking
speech therapy, 64
Stark-Vance, Virginia, 25, 33, 41, 43, 60
statistics, 9, 28, 61, 78
  cigarette smoking relationship to brain tumors, 25–26
  headaches, 31, 33
stereotactic radiosurgery, 50–52
support groups, 69
surgery, 45, 49, 56
  location of tumor and, 45–46
  procedures involved in, 46–48
  technology advances in, 77–79
survivor's guilt, 66
symptoms
  difficulty in distinguishing, 30–31, 36
  headaches, 8, 31–33
  location of brain tumor and, 34–35
  nausea, 31, 33
  seizures, 33–34
targeted therapies, 84–85

technological advances
  chemotherapy, 83–86
  gene therapy, 86–87
  general information about, 75–77
  immunotherapy, 87–89
  radiotherapy, 79–84
  surgery, 77–79
telomerase, 87
Temodar, 75
Thalidomide, 86
transsphenoidal surgery, 49
Tribolet, Nicholas de, 74
tumor formation process, 22–23

vaccinations, 87–89
vectors, 86–87
ventricles, 18, 21
viruses, 24–25, 86–87
vocational assistance, 64–65
vomiting, 31, 33

Wernicke, Carl, 37
World Health Organization, 16

X-rays, 38, 41

Zeltzer, Paul, 14, 22, 61, 69

Picture Credits

Cover photo: S. Fraser, RVI/Photo Researchers, Inc.
Maury Aaseng, 16, 20, 21, 26, 27, 81, 83
AP/Wide World Photos, 24, 41, 51, 58, 61, 71, 73, 76, 89
© Marc Asnin/CORBIS, 13
John Bavosi/Photo Researchers, Inc., 54
Neil Borden/Photo Researchers, Inc., 15
Simon Frasier/RNC, Newcastle upon Tyne/Photo Researchers,
     Inc., 31
© Rick Friedman/CORBIS (both photos), 79
Hulton Archive/Getty images, 36
© Janine Wiedel Photolibrary/Alamy, 68
Nancy Kedersha/Ucla/Photo Researchers, Inc., 19
© Helen King/CORBIS, 48
© LWA–Dan Tardif/CORBIS, 62
Photos.com, 25, 32, 42
© Roger Ressmeyer/CORBIS, 47
© Greg Smith/CORBIS, 85
© Howard Sochurek/CORBIS, 9
Javier Soriano/AFP/Getty Images, 10
Jeff Tomkinson/Photo Researchers, Inc., 35

About the Author

Arda Darakjian Clark holds a master's degree in English. She has worked for many years as a technical writer, writing procedure and system user manuals. She has also worked on various projects as a freelance writer and editor. She is the author of *Dyslexia* in this series of books. She lives in Redondo Beach, California, with her husband and children.